DO
NOT
COMPLY

DO
NOT
COMPLY

Taking Power Back from America's Corrupt Elite

WILL WITT

CENTER
STREET

New York • Nashville

Center Street
Hachette Book Group
1290 Avenue of the Americas, New York, NY 10104
centerstreet.com
twitter.com/centerstreet

First Edition: September 2023

Center Street is a division of Hachette Book Group, Inc. The Center Street name and logo are trademarks of Hachette Book Group, Inc.

The publisher is not responsible for websites (or their content) that are not owned by the publisher.

The Hachette Speakers Bureau provides a wide range of authors for speaking events. To find out more, go to hachettespeakersbureau.com or email HachetteSpeakers@hbgusa.com.

Center Street books may be purchased in bulk for business, educational, or promotional use. For information, please contact your local bookseller or the Hachette Book Group Special Markets Department at special.markets@hbgusa.com.

Library of Congress Cataloging-in-Publication Data has been applied for.

ISBNs: 9781546005582 (hardcover), 9781546005605 (ebook)

Printed in the United States of America

LAKE

10 9 8 7 6 5 4 3 2 1

To my pastor, mentor, and friend Jake.
Who showed me what real loyalty is,
believed in me like no one else, and became
the father to me I never had.

CONTENTS

FOREWORD

By Dennis Prager

Will Witt gets it.

He understands what has happened to the greatest country ever created—the freest by far, the most affluent by far, the country that has given more opportunity to more people from more backgrounds, again by far.

As he puts it in his introduction, the "idea of America is dead, and we have killed her. The remnants of her great past live on in history books and nostalgic conversation, but the soul of America lies in a casket."

That a young American writes such a thing should make grown men weep. I have lived more than forty years more than Will has, and I often run a debate in my mind: Who has it worse—people my age who lived almost our entire lives in a great country and now see it being destroyed by its own citizens, or Americans of Will's age who might never experience the great country older Americans were so fortunate to inherit?

The answer is unknowable. It is not exactly like the famous question of whether it is better to have loved and lost or not to have loved at all. Everyone who loves knows they will lose that love; given that death is inevitable, they or the one(s) they love will die. But the death of America—as an idea, which is really all America ever was—is not inevitable. And certainly not so soon. Perhaps after a millennium or even 500 years. But after less than 250 years?

Will lays out the issues clearly and concisely. That is no small feat for anyone, especially someone as young as he is. But wisdom and clarity (are they even different qualities?) are not confined to any age. As I wrote in one of my columns, I and most of my fellow students at my yeshiva high school (a Jewish school with a rigorous religious education) had more wisdom than do the faculty members of any elite American university today.

In addition to wisdom, Will has courage, which, along with wisdom, is the most important human quality. Many people have good intentions, but good intentions without wisdom, let alone courage, not only do not lead to good; they lead to evil. Many people with good intentions supported communism, the greatest mass-murder ideology in history. And at this time, many Americans with good intentions support the left, the ideology that is destroying America.

But Will has more than wisdom and courage. He has the ability—as rare as wisdom and courage—to explain. The tragedy of the modern age is that most Christians and Jews did not explain the need for God and the Bible, and most Americans did not explain America.

That's why this is an important book. It explains our

current crisis. And, remarkably, it also teaches the reader an immense amount due to the prodigious amount of reading and research that went into it.

As it happens, I agree with Will's takes on almost every issue he covers. On rare occasions we differ. I support billions in aid to Ukraine because a great country with the greatest strength cannot just watch a malevolent power with nuclear weapons conquer another country (though we should be pursuing peace with just as much fervor). And I have a slightly more favorable view of the Republican Party, if only because it is the only alternative to the America-destroying Democratic Party. But those differences don't matter. For one thing, if I only read books with which I completely agree, I would read no books. For another, Will's differing positions are so well supported, I need to confront them.

I could go on at great length. But this is Will's book, not mine. I would only add that Will has a heart as big as his intellect. As an example, he writes here:

"Communism is an insidious ideology that over the last century killed over a hundred million people. That is a truly unquantifiable number, especially when you take into consideration not just the deaths, but the wounded, the raped, the sick, and all of the other millions affected: mothers separated from their children, husbands who lost their wives, and friends who would never see each other again."

Too few people write about the unfathomable evils of communism, and among those who do, most mention only the death count—which is certainly vital to bring up. But it takes a special heart and mind to note, as Will does, the exponential suffering of those not murdered.

Will Witt is a special man who has written a special book in a dark time.

DO
NOT
COMPLY

AMERICAN REALITY

A nation of sheep will beget a government of wolves.

—Edward R. Murrow

A merica. The greatest country ever created. A place where you could come from nothing, and become anything. A country of freedom, but of law and order. A country that other nations around the world aspired to be. A country of great culture, with a history full of struggles and beauty. A country that seemed to always be striving for greater heights despite all the odds against it. A place where great discussions and thinkers abounded who would come to learn and teach to inspire and cultivate the world. A nation of fearless leaders and stalwarts who did the right thing even if it was difficult to do so. A country where your voice and your vote meant something. A country of soldiers who fought every battle with bravery and heroism. A country that saved the world. A country whose innovation and wealth were unmatched, whose exploits and inventions drove the carriage of history forward.

A country that garnered respect from all corners of the earth. A country its people loved. A country its people were proud of. A country people would die for.

This idea of America is dead, and we have killed her. The remnants of her great past live on in history books and nostalgic conversation, but the soul of America lies in a casket, buried beneath the steps of Washington, D.C. We as a people have allowed our country to be taken over by traitors and tyrants, weak and lazy men, and godless liars and false idols. The people at the very pinnacles of our society have sold us, the American people, out for their own avarice and selfishness whenever it benefited them, and have done it all under the guise of "progress," or "strength," or "patriotism." They put your devotion to our nation under question for battling against their greed, and present you as the sinner for doubting the quality of their intentions. You are deemed as disloyal for not accepting the death of your nation, and thus many turn a blind eye, letting the rot of our elite fester over the United States. The stench of America's soul decomposing beneath the Capitol is perfume to the people who work there.

The America you grew up in is no longer here. But what is easier: Telling the truth about the reality of our country, or keeping up the lie that everything is okay? Our country is in sharp decline in all of the metrics that truly matter, yet we often fail to truly call out the culprits responsible for it. And who are these corrupters of our great country? Well, they are politicians, they are businessmen, they are celebrities, they are media executives, they are scientists, they are pastors, they are teachers, they are parents. They are the most elite and wealthy people in our society, and they are our next-door neighbors. They are of all races, all religions, from all around the world. They are Republicans, they are Democrats. They are the World Economic Forum, they are your second grader's science teacher. They are *everywhere*. America has fallen into decay, not just because of our leaders and the oligarchy controlling us, but because the American people have forgotten what this country, and our humanity, are supposed to look like.

Over the course of history, every great civilization has collapsed at some point or another, and for a variety of reasons. Conquest, internal strife, disease; there are a myriad of reasons always lurking around the corner threatening empires with destruction. Ancient Rome, perhaps the greatest civilization ever to exist, is no different, and its rise, stagnation, and eventual fall are eerily similar to the story of America and the condition our country is in at this very moment, with all of the same apparent warning signs. In the second century, the wealth gap between Rome's rich and the poor grew enormously, creating income inequality between the lower and upper classes.[1] The middle class was being destroyed, and the wealth gap grew. This led to too many poor people, whom the government could not control or provide for. The government decided eventually that it must deal with this crisis, and reforms by Gaius Gracchus, the brother of Tiberius, who was a victim of growing political violence and assassinations in Rome, instituted grain subsidies for the citizens of Rome, turning the empire into a welfare state.[2] The people of Rome became accustomed to their *panem et circenses* (bread and circuses), and politicians who promised more and more free handouts to the citizens were almost always the most popular.[3]

But this would all come to ruin as the Roman government went bankrupt over welfare programs and massive military spending, steeply devaluing the currency, which led to hyperinflation all across the empire. This meant a further rise in taxes and price controls to pay for all the debt the empire had accumulated, and much of Rome's poor could not afford this increase in taxation, many being sold into slavery when they could no longer pay the state their due.[4] Many of the Roman lower class actually welcomed the invasion of the barbarian hordes in the fifth century, seeing it as a way out from under the thumb of the massive taxes levied by the Roman Empire.

Ancient Rome also imported huge numbers of people from outside the empire into their country and military, many of whom would never assimilate fully into Roman life.[5] This further fractured Rome's culture and demographics, with a "melting pot" of competing tribes and peoples, often with very different customs and ways of culture than the true-born Roman citizens. Then came the decadence of the ancient Roman Empire, and its fall into immorality. Weak leaders and weak men were everywhere, and eventually they were conquered. The Western Empire collapsed, ushering in the so-called dark ages.

How does America stack up? Well, we have a massive welfare state, with the country's welfare spending tripling over the last twenty years.[6] In 2023, the American government is projected to spend $1.3 trillion on welfare, or 22 percent of our entire national budget.[7] We have created a nation of people who no longer need to rely on any sort of work ethic or merit, but can just count on the state to provide for every need they may have, further exacerbating the weakening of society. We also spend incredibly heavily, and unnecessarily, on our military budget as ancient Rome did, a massive $1.1 trillion annually.[8] As Rome expanded, ever increasing its empire in history's first real attempt at globalization, it also struggled to control such a massive landmass. In America's case, we send weapons and military aid all around the world, building up the military-industrial complex and making defense contractors incredibly rich. Does $50 billion to Ukraine really seem like the most pertinent use of American taxpayer dollars when our country is crumbling from the inside?[9] I don't think so. America, and much of Western Europe, for that matter, also lets in hundreds of thousands of illegal migrants and refugees, often from cultures inferior to our own. Many of these migrants are unskilled single men spreading values antithetical to those of the West.[10] Some commit crimes.[11] Many end up getting handouts from the government.[12] Furthermore, our country is in a crisis of strength and meaning, and some of the abhorrent ancient practices of ancient Rome's decadence are manifest today, such as the sexualization of children. It was quite common in Rome, and even more so in ancient Greece, to partake in pederasty, or the act of sexual activity between men and young boys.[13] Look at the West today, with the downplaying of pedophilia, the sexualization of children with radical gender and sexual orientation ideologies, and the sheer scope of the child sex trafficking industry in America.[14] What the left is doing to children is evil, and as societies become more comfortable with the sexualization of children and the tearing apart of the innocence of youth, the only outcome for that aforementioned society is a complete dissolution of social cohesion and morality.

Ancient Rome fell for many reasons; some may not be completely akin to ours, and many of the main points of its collapse are still heavily debated today. Our Western world today may not have barbarian invaders, gladiator fights, and polytheistic religions, but when you look at the decay of empires, the signs reflect the same visage as America's now. We live in a society with massive debt, controlled by a selfish oligarchy dictating our speech and actions through soft despotism, with a lack of reverence for cultural heritage and religion, and a fractured and splintered people with little to no purpose, and no binding framework or values to fold them in together. Our middle class is being ravaged and destroyed by a corrupt ruling class that wants to turn us into the next generation of peasants. We live in the individualism monolith, where there is no real sense of community, but we all live nearly identical lives, all according to the design of the world controllers and their lackeys. During the time of the American colonists, roughly 90 percent were self-sufficient farmers, able to provide for themselves and live a life of freedom. Today, 58 percent of Americans have less than $1,000 in the bank, and almost half don't have a net worth of even $10,000 by the time they die.[15]

Today, Millennials in America own only 3 percent of the nation's wealth.[16] Compare this to baby boomers at the same age, around the year 1989, who owned 21 percent of the nation's wealth. Millennials also shoulder a disproportionate share of the nation's liabilities, coming in at 16 percent. What would normally define adulthood—marriage, children, and owning a house—is happening less and less for the Millennial generation, due to a variety of factors. The price of education has skyrocketed, way past the rate of inflation, and Americans are taking on massive amounts of debt to get their diplomas, if they even finish. Housing has also become much more expensive. Only 39 percent of people aged twenty-five to thirty-four own their home in America. In 2004, 70 percent of Americans owned their home, while today that number is only 63 percent, and dropping fast. Millennials are also getting married and having children later and at lower rates than we have seen in thirty-two years, creating a Peter Pan lifestyle among young people and further eroding the familial and communal values our country was built on.[17] Marriage is also an indicator of wealth, with married people on average making more money than those who are single, which is shown by the fact that Millennials today are earning lower wages and making less money than previous generations. In 1960, 70 percent of American families relied on only one income earner. In 2020 this was down to 30 percent. From 1950 to 2019 the average age of first marriage for men and women rose by seven years. In the 1970s, women had their first child by the age of twenty-one; today that age is twenty-seven. In 2016 there were only 62.5 births per 1,000 women. We are at a tipping point in the West. If we do not pick up the pace on marriages and children, we will be facing a massive population deficit, with not enough children to fuel this nation, pay into Social Security, provide for the elderly, and keep America's dominance on the world stage secure.

Small businesses in this country are also falling behind, as mega-corporations are working hand in hand with government to monopolize our country. Why is it that during the Covid lockdowns small businesses had to close their doors while massive corporations were allowed to stay open? By June 2021, over a third of U.S. small businesses had shut their doors.[18] The point is that they don't want you to be self-sufficient. They want you to be dependent on the state and the mega-corporations for all your needs. The government and corporations maliciously work together to dry up any sort of competition that threatens their reign of power and domination, and attack small businesses as much as possible to further their consumer empire. Large corporations lobby the government for regulations and tax increases, paying off the politicians for favors, and these favors, always implemented through fancy phrases such as "saving democracy" or "build back better," stifle small businesses and competition while allowing the mega-companies to thrive.

Our government doesn't work for the people. It works for greed, money, and power, and kicks the American people while they're down any chance it can get. And this is not just a Democrat issue. It is on both sides of the political aisle, and both parties are guilty of selling out the American people. No wonder so many people are apathetic about politics and voting in this country when election integrity seems to be at an all-time low and your country's politicians are nothing more than slaves to the corporations, ready to be bought and sold by the highest bidder. It is also no wonder, then, why nothing ever gets done that actually benefits the American people, and how every new piece of legislation or "progressive" reform is merely a way for the government and lobbyists to line their pockets. Our political system is an absolute joke, and I hate to say it, but if you are holding out hope for your favorite political party to break free from this, or feel your favorite politician is infallible and won't succumb to this corruption, you unfortunately are gravely mistaken. Our system works on the premise that everyone plays the same game, and if you choose to rebel, then you don't get to play.

If the French Revolution taught us anything, it is that when the leaders of a citizenry live decadent lifestyles, exploiting the general population, things usually go sour for the society as a whole. When the Parisian peasants walked by the aristocracy's homes and saw their "leaders" getting drunk and partying luxuriously while they were taxed to death to pay for these soirees, an urge for revolution boiled inside them. And that is exactly what happened. The people rose up, the ruling class was chastised, and in a matter of months the monarchy's heads no longer rested on opulent pillows in grand bedrooms but on spikes after being chopped off by the guillotine.

We are controlled by an oligarchy. Your constitutional republic is gone. You have been positively coerced into believing you are free while you are distracted with mindless entertainment, instant communication, welfare, "advanced" medical care, and endless food variety, all sweeping your mind away from the real problems at hand. Economically we are collapsing, and future generations won't be able to sustain the burden we have put on them. Culturally we are vapid and empty, with little to connect one person to the next aside from their love of consumerism and cheap entertainment. Technologically, we are at our apex, yet we are creating tools and inventions that destroy our humanity and exacerbate our vanity, idolizing ourselves as new gods.

I hate to be so cynical. I would love to just tell you about the victories and triumphs taking place in America today. But I believe it to be much more important to tell you all about the problems facing our country and world. Because if we don't recognize the problems at hand, can we truly ever fix them? If we choose to ignore the reality of our situation, are we really better off in blind ignorance? In truth, we cannot be. It is time to come to the realization that both of our political parties and our political system are corrupt and broken and need to be completely overhauled. We cannot keep idly pretending as if the difference between a Republican and Democrat in office is all that great, and that a politician is going to miraculously save us. Power lies where people believe it lies, and so as long as we continue to believe it is with these selfish rulers and their diktats, we will forever be oppressed and dominated by their will.

We can't keep acting as if the elites in control of us are stupid. They are smarter than you know and commit evil for their own benefit. We can't continue to think facts and logic are going to save us when those in power laugh at the hypocrisy of their actions and roll over us anyway. We cannot continue to think we are free just because we live in America. We have taken it for granted, and thus we have lost it without even realizing it. We have been taken advantage of and lied to every step of the way, and I am done with the lies. I support an America that was, but not the America that is, because it is no longer recognizable from the country that was fought for on this land all those hundreds of years ago. Until we restore those tenets and those values, we don't live in America. We live in a play-pretend America, with illusions of what the West is supposed to look like, which in reality is nothing more than a funhouse mirror.

So what do we do? Am I writing this book just to tell you all how hopeless and futile our struggles and lives are in America today? How we can never live up to our glorious past and our future is destined for darkness? That you are merely a slave and your circumstances are dire and unchangeable no matter what you do about it? No. That is not why I wrote this book. I spent months researching and writing and editing this work to show you the truth about the situation the West has put itself in, and how we, as individuals, can escape from it. The first half of this book declares the ills plaguing us, how we got here, and who is responsible for the state of America and its decline. The second half is the antidote I have found to escape as a society, as families, and as people from the current state of our world and the dystopian future we could very well have in store.

Haldir says in *The Lord of the Rings*, "The world is indeed full of peril, and in it there are many dark places; but still there is much that is fair, and though in all lands love is now mingled with grief, it grows perhaps the greater." It is easy to despair on the failings of our world, the evil we see around us, and the absence of light. But in all dark places there is beauty too, and we cannot be subdued by sadness and weakness despite the outlook of our troubles. If all seems hopeless and all looks as if it is lost, you can be the fire that brightens the doom that surrounds you. Don't rely on others to fix the abounding corruption or slay the demons that dwell inside you; instead, wear the armor of God, have hope, and shine as a light in dark places, that illuminates ever brighter when all other lights go out.

Your only choice out of this is to not comply with their tyranny. When the people stop living by the tenets of these new self-proclaimed deities and start living by the rules of God and their own individuality, only then can we improve our lot. When the elites realize they can no longer whip us into submission to serve as their conduits for more power and wealth, only then will America return to the place it once was. A place where the greedy and evil and diabolical were afraid to show their faces.

Chapter 1

A BRAVE NEW WORLD

It seems to me that the nature of the ultimate
revolution with which we are now faced is precisely this:
That we are in the process of developing a whole series
of techniques which will enable the controlling
oligarchy who have always existed and will always
exist to get people to love their servitude.

—*Aldous Huxley*

If the fascist and communist dictatorships of the twentieth century taught us anything, it is that tyranny induced by violence and force is short-lived and catastrophic. Like a supernova, these types of totalitarian regimes begin in a flurry of fire, with large-scale government control and brainwashing followed by horrific carnage and death. But as quickly and as sweeping as they begin, they burn out into utter futility and destruction. Most dictatorships do not last for more than seventy years, and most are far shorter than that. Eventually the citizens realize they don't like to be controlled or lied to and revolt, the system crashes under its own weight, or a larger and stronger nation comes and saves the day. Whatever the circumstance of its demise, it is clear that tyranny where a select few violently oppress the many cannot be sustained over long periods. If you persecute, starve, and kill off your people, become a pariah on the world stage, and your country has run out of money, you have no choice but to watch your society collapse.

It doesn't take an expert on communism to know that sending millions of your own people to the gulags is not a sustainable way to keep your country in a viable economic and social state. But what would happen if you made it so people *liked* going to the gulags? I'm not talking about people lying through their teeth to their government with a fake smile *claiming* they love the Siberian work camps; I am talking about citizens actually enjoying the shackles that are placed on them. What would happen if you made millions of people actually believe that the oppression and diktats enforced on them were good for them, and they learned to love their servitude? This idea of fooling your own populace into loving slavery and hating freedom is the epitome of Aldous Huxley's 1932 novel *Brave New World*, and is the driving force behind the means by which leaders of the twenty-first century have carried out their dominion over their people.

Frederick Douglass was a slave turned abolitionist who was able to escape his masters in 1838 after boarding a northbound train with the help of his love Anna Murray. Douglass, to many people's surprise, ended up becoming a prolific author and orator who was able to influence thousands on the evils and immoral nature of slavery in America. In his first autobiography, *Narrative of the Life of Frederick Douglass, an American Slave* (1845), Douglass remarked on slavery, "I have found that, to make a contented slave, it is necessary to make a thoughtless one…He must be able to detect no inconsistencies in slavery; he must be made to feel that slavery is right; and he can be brought to that only when he ceases to be a man." This idea reaches beyond just the Africans brought over in the slave trade and into the essence of what it means to be a slave. Slavery can be defined as a person who is controlled by something or someone. In *Brave New World*, the people of the novel do not even know that they are slaves to the world controllers. They truly believe their actions are not part of some greater control, that they are living wonderful lives, and that human existence is supposed to be that way. They are, to paraphrase Frederick Douglass, "contented slaves."

So the question is, how does one make a contented slave? How does a society come to appreciate its servitude and new feudalism? The first part of the plan involves convincing the people of your society that they have freedom and agency to decide their own fates, when in reality their choices are manufactured and processed by the people in control. You think you're making a choice at the polls for a Democrat or a Republican? Wait until you find out where both parties get their campaign financing from. You think you're making a conscious decision about the restaurant you decide to dine at? Turns out all the restaurants are owned by the same people, with food shipped in from the same billion-dollar mega–factory farms. You think the city you live in is so unique? Look at the architecture, the layout, the types of jobs and companies and tell me again how distinct it is. The illusion of choice is the leader in the formation of a slave population. Sure, you can choose Miller over Budweiser, Google Chrome over Safari, a Toyota over a Honda, but the miniscule choices you make are only mere distractions from the fact that the larger decisions of your life are fabricated as part of a masquerade to keep you docile and contented. Everyone lives the same existence as the person next door, with minute discrepancies in personal choice that really are no choice at all, keeping you inoculated in the culture the oligarchy manufactures. In an age of such decadence and comfort, great intellect and meaning is lost, and the corporate and bureaucratic powers keep us satisfied through consumerism and cheap vanity.

Once you have created a population that believes they are autonomous, the next step is to condition them with drugs and vices. In *Brave New World*, this is done through soma, a recreational drug that keeps the people of the novel always happy and stimulated. Soma also serves the purpose of keeping them compliant and unaware of the evils and domination of the world controllers, and makes them never question who is actually running the show. Think back to America now, and look at the people addicted to drugs and alcohol in this country. Over twenty-one million Americans suffer from at least one addiction, and addiction costs our country over $600 billion per year, and it is only getting worse.[1] Since 1990, drug overdose deaths in America have tripled, and one in three families is affected in some way by addiction.[2] Culturally, drugs and alcohol are pushed as an escape from reality and the key to a fun time, and thus a nation of users and addicts is born. The biggest musical acts in this country focus on partying and drug abuse in their songs and herald them as a way to have fun, instead of something to stay away from that could destroy your life. Then you have Big Pharma producing highly addictive and dangerous drugs with an army of doctors prescribing them to people who don't even need them, further exacerbating the problem. Millions more people who aren't addicted to drugs or alcohol still abuse them heavily, creating a dumbed-down and intoxicated populace that is susceptible to more vices and political apathy, because its worries lie in partying, vanity, and dependence, not on meaning, the happenings of the world around them, or society at large.[3] The concoction of positive reinforcement when it comes to drug and alcohol use is the next step toward contented slavery, and a nation that cannot think clearly due to its use of substances is bound to be controlled and oppressed.

In addition to substance abuse, people in America, as in the novel, are constantly supplied with endless distractions that keep them blind to the works of control placed upon them. In *Brave New World* this comes in the form of mundane and obscene acts and material that serve as a constant form of easy "pleasure." With pleasure and distraction abounding, the people of the novel never trouble themselves with greater issues taking place around them, and why would they? If your life is so easy and pleasurable that you never have to worry about any grander purpose, then the majority of people will choose that safety over breaking out of the system nine times out of ten. The situation in America is eerily similar. Social media serves as a means of constant cheap entertainment and vanity that keeps us inundated with mostly nonsense for hours on end. An estimated 420 million people around the world suffered from internet addiction in 2022, and that number is constantly growing.[4] Some teenagers spend up to nine hours a day on social media, so it becomes no wonder why we have one of the most isolated and lonely generations coming up with Generation Z. Social media creates a self-obsessed and narcissistic people, who place themselves at the center of attention of every discourse due to the fact they are constantly worried about likes and engagement on their profiles. It creates a dopamine feedback loop that turns people into obsessive and self-absorbed addicts who are oblivious to all else around them that moves. Then you consider the content on the platforms, which is mostly vapid, pornographic, or superfluous, and you have a population of zombies, eyes constantly glued to a screen with no worries of the greater world at large because the only world that matters is *their* small electronic world of pleasure.

Now that your population *believes* they are free, are drunk and high, and have constant pleasure and distractions, what is next? Now you move on to the most important step in this process of control, and that is positive reinforcement. As the American psychologist B. F. Skinner noted, "Now that we know how positive reinforcement works, and why negative doesn't, we can be more deliberate, and hence more successful, in our cultural design. We can achieve a sort of control under which the controlled... nevertheless feel free. They are doing what they want to do, not what they are forced to do. That's the source of the tremendous power of positive reinforcement—there's no restraint and no revolt. By a careful design, we control not the final behavior, but the inclination to behave—the motives, the desires, the wishes. The curious thing is that in that case the question of freedom never arises."

If you hit a dog for barking at the window, he may stop for a moment, but once you leave, he will go on barking. Now, if you give a dog a bone for *not* barking, he will always come back to you without a sound, wanting another treat. This is the epitome of positive reinforcement, the means of conditioning people into their actions through the promise of reward. Negative behaviors are applauded in *Brave New World*, whereas thinking for yourself or being moral is punished and seen as wrong. People's vices, their lust, their drug use, and their complacency are rewarded in the novel and seen as freedom, whereas those who don't engage in those activities are ostracized and belittled by those around them.

It is easy to look at our world today and wonder why so many people who engage in terrible behaviors seem to be at the apex of our system. Some of the most evil people in the world are in some of the highest places in our society. From greedy businessmen to conniving politicians to impious pastors to arrogant celebrities, many of the most prestigious institutions in America have now become dominated by debauchery, avarice, and malice. And it seems to only be getting worse as time goes on. While many governments across the world have ascribed to a wholly tyrannical agenda, our culture is filled with vapid nonsense, and many of the people who are supposed to defend our nation have turned instead to egotism and self-idolatry. We live in a world where people who intentionally sin for their own wealth and grandeur are not chastised, but instead are given awards and honors. After calling for the dismantling of the police and rioting and looting throughout America, Black Lives Matter was nominated for the Nobel Peace Prize. National Geographic made a documentary showcasing Dr. Anthony Fauci's triumphs. Megan Thee Stallion, a female rapper who claims to be "on her thot shit," won Best New Artist at the 2021 Grammys. But you have to realize that this is all according to plan. The way of the wicked prospers, the ones who act akin to everyone else are safe, and the tallest blade of grass gets cut first.

In the Western world today, we are in a moral crisis and a struggle for meaning like no other time in human history because of the feedback loop of negative and positive behaviors. Imagine the young Christian man who wants to live a life for Christ, of real masculinity, and for truth. All the while he does this, the vultures around him snicker at his decisions. They laugh and mock the way he chooses to live, all reinforced by the modern zeitgeist that religion is a farce. He eventually becomes shunned by everyone around him, and he succumbs to the way our culture has been designed. Instead of being a leader or denying the ways of those around him and fighting against the prevalent customs of our age, he falters and joins in the ranks of those who get rewarded for their laziness, their collectivism, and their immorality. This is just one example among many, but it serves as a lesson to remind you that staying within the box that our culture has created around you is the key to the artificial positivity that drives our society. Whether you are a bold and new artist, a free thinker of ideas and concepts, a preserver of history and heritage, or someone who just doesn't fit the mold of the typical societal paradigm, you will receive backlash, vitriol, and condemnation from others and the grander world at large for daring to think out of the scope of the shackles placed upon you.

This mockery, laziness, and safety of the "herd," as Nietzsche would call them, serves the purpose to the world controllers in that they have created a docile, dumbed-down, and simple-to-control population. If an individual is chastised for being a free thinker by his fellow citizens, it keeps that individual in his place. If the media attacks anyone with a difference of opinion, people will be much less likely to publish or say anything novel out of fear of being destroyed. In my time doing hundreds of man-on-the-street videos for PragerU and speaking to thousands of people on all sorts of topics, it is quite clear that most people's opinions and thoughts, especially young people's, are incredibly shallow. They have been given ideas, safe thoughts that keep them in line with what their friends believe and what is acceptable on their Twitter timelines, but have not pondered much about the implications or deeper meaning behind them. So out of fear of being "different" from their peers, they make war against anyone who dares to say something out of their scope of understanding to make sure no one is different. It is a system that protects itself. The world controllers design a system of anti-morals and ways to think, and the masses devour them and shun anyone who deviates. There is safety and assurance in feeling like you are part of a group. There is no comfort in feeling alone. Most people choose the first option.

This is not a left-or-right issue. In the conservative lexicon, just as much as in the left's discussions, there are "approved" messages, conversations, and theories. Yes, conservatism is on the back foot of the left's dominance in America, but tell me, have you as a conservative ever felt afraid to say something for fear of being ostracized by other conservatives? When the Covid vaccine first came out, I remember feeling like one of the only ones who was speaking about whether or not these new mRNA injections might have some complications, both in the safety of the shot and the mandates that came with them. I was slandered by many a conservative (and leftist, for that matter) for my "anti-science" and conspiratorial messaging. I got labeled as "far right" even by those on the right, and lost opportunities that other, "safer" conservatives would now get due to my stances and thoughts. For me, that sort of labeling and shaming never affected my mindset, but I do this for a living. For someone whose living depends on anything else, a difference of opinion could mean losing your job, your friends, or your family, and that is all by design. The oligarchy demoralizes you by taking everything away from you for breaking your chains.

It is rumored that the CIA used the term "conspiracy theorist" in 1964 to culturally ostracize people who thought outside the accepted narrative on the Kennedy assassination.[5] Now, I don't know whether that is the case or not, but it is abundantly clear that terms like "conspiracy theorist" are thrown at anyone with reckless abandon to try and discredit and divide them. Our world is dominated by slander and shaming instead of questioning and discussion. Instead of pursuing what is true, we pursue what is safe, and that is irrelevant to political parties. To be a real free thinker and break, you can't think in terms of just political parties, you have to think in terms of what is true.

This is the "brave new world" that we now reside in. A society dominated by sin and perversion, where there is no moral compass because morality is relegated to a relic of the past in the subjective-truth world we live in. A society where technology is at its peak, but where meaning is at its lowest. A society where anything is possible, as long as it's deemed okay by the oligarchy. The fight to restore America and freedom is about more than your political compass, an economic system, or a formation of government. This is a full frontal assault on your humanity, where the consequence of losing is a life of bondage. A bondage where you believe you are free, but all the while play into the hands of the people at the top. Your actions and movements are guided by the invisible puppeteer's hand, slowly stringing you along to your cell of complacency. According to the world controllers, the only real sin in this world is thinking differently than everyone else, and if that is the case, the only way we get out of this is by sinning by their standards ferociously.

Chapter 2

AMERICA'S POLITICAL SYSTEM

Of course the people don't want war. But after all,
it's the leaders of the country who determine the policy,
and it's always a simple matter to drag the people
along whether it's a democracy, a fascist dictatorship,
or a parliament, or a communist dictatorship.
Voice or no voice, the people can always be brought
to the bidding of the leaders. That is easy. All you
have to do is tell them they are being attacked,
and denounce the pacifists for lack of patriotism,
and exposing the country to greater danger.

—Hermann Goering at the Nuremberg trials

Alexis de Tocqueville, a French aristocrat and writer, warned in his 1840 work *Democracy in America* that our country could very well be heading into what he called "soft despotism" if certain government and social actions took place. He noted, "After having thus taken each individual one by one into its powerful hands, and having molded him as it pleases, the sovereign power extends its arms over the entire society; it covers the surface of society with a network of small, complicated, minute, and uniform rules, which the most original minds and the most vigorous souls cannot break through to go beyond the crowd; it does not break wills, but it softens them, bends them and directs them; it rarely forces action, but it constantly opposes your acting; it does not destroy, it prevents birth; it does not tyrannize, it hinders, it represses, it enervates, it extinguishes, it stupefies, and finally it reduces each nation to being nothing more than a flock of timid and industrious animals, of which the government is the shepherd." The essence of what he warns about is a massive administrative state, where the government holds all the power and the people are treated as a herd, rather than individuals with their own liberty, motives, and freedoms. The government grinds its gears of bureaucracy and keeps its people always safe but destitute for the cravings of their soul. Hmm, does that remind you at all of any novel we have previously discussed?

Have you heard of the paradox of Theseus's ship? The thought goes something like this: Theseus has a ship, and eventually many of the wooden planks and pieces of the vessel get worn down and rot. One by one, all of the pieces are replaced over time until every piece of the ship is now new and none of the original parts remain. So, the question is: Is this still Theseus's ship? Or is it a new ship entirely?

I pondered this paradox in the context of America. Is America still America, even if the original ideals of the country are replaced? Or is it now a totally new entity, no longer recognizable from its primary founding and creation? Is America still a country because of what it was intended to be? Or is it America because of what it is now? Is it still America if the First Amendment is shattered, now wielded at the whim of Big Tech overlords? Is it still America if our Christian foundation is replaced with anti-history and nihilism? Is it still America if our "American dream" is dead and our citizens are serfs to the ruling class and massive corporations? Is it still America if our constitutional republic is seized by a bloated bureaucracy and fraudulent voting system? Is it still America if our non-interventionism is replaced by money laundering and greedy warmongering? Is it still America if our people still believe that it is? Or is it just a nostalgic feeling that only serves as a reminder of a more magnificent past?

America. Is it just the name that remains?

Compared to our country's founding, or even fifty years ago, America is in many ways unrecognizable from what it once was. Its government and political system are but a mere shadow of what our founders intended for our republic. The Declaration of Independence was inspired by the Dutch and their republic, and was intended to be a government by the people, for the people, with its major tenet being limited state power that had checks and balances to keep all three branches of government accountable.[1] Now the only checks are the ones going from pocket to pocket, lobbyist to politician, and super PAC to campaign. Crisis after crisis takes place in America, and each time, the government grows larger and larger, until we are now left with an unrecognizable behemoth of a state that is exactly what Tocqueville warned us about.

From 1900 to 1980, the American government grew three- to sixfold by all quantitative measures, and is continuing to grow ever more.[2] This does not even include all the ways the government has increased in its scope that cannot be measured statistically, as in all the ways the government has seized powers over institutions and purviews that never belonged to it before. Social Security, finance, health care, defense, student loans, and basically everything you need to live is now in some way or another controlled wholly or in part by the government. Long gone are the days of a free market, businesses rising and falling as demand and advancements in technology adapt and change. Now you have a state that monitors, oversees, and bails out corporations and special interests, creating a soft socialism where the government in many respects controls the means of production. It is easy to think you live in some capitalist utopia when around you is a never-ending supply of restaurants, hotels, and shops and you are just a consumer. But it is hard to believe you don't live in a socialist monopoly when you try to start a small business to rival any of the massive ones you see.

How did this all come to pass? How did our government start performing merely on the whims of corporations and special interests and disregard the American people and their liberties? The answer is clear: political contributions and lobbying. In 2021 alone, the U.S. Chamber of Commerce spent $66 million on lobbying, and more is on the way.[3] In 2019, lobbyists spent $3.4 billion on political lobbying alone.[4] Lobbying in its current state is protected by the First Amendment; people are allowed the right to petition their government, and that essentially is what lobbying is at its most basic level. Lobbying is supposed to be a totally legitimate form of government balance, where the citizens of the country ask the government for what they want in order to keep the politicians aware of their needs and concerns.

Not all lobbying is a great evil that must be eradicated at all costs. But the problem with lobbying is that it is very easily influenced and dominated by human nature. Lobbying is the *one ring to rule them all*, if you will, where on its own it can do nothing, but when it is given to men, they are easily destroyed by the greed and power they now possess. Mega-corporations use lobbying as a means to an end. It has been transformed entirely into a way to buy off politicians, promising them money and rewards in exchange for special privileges and legislation. Often it's legislation that snuffs out competition and rarely helps the citizens that lobbying is supposed to protect, only serving the interest of whatever company is doing the lobbying. Politicians, being easily corrupted and bought out, often take the money without a second thought, doing the bidding of whoever writes them the biggest check. It is legal bribery. Our government officials are nothing more than slaves to the corporations, where lobbyists buy who they know will do their will, making the politicians, for lack of a better word, their bitches.

Here is an example. In 2017, FedEx spent $10 million lobbying the federal government. Much of that lobbying was geared toward a tax cut bill that would benefit FedEx.[5] In 2018, FedEx got their way, and ended up saving $1.6 billion on taxes. If lobbying was fair across the board, with all interest groups equally represented, this would not be an issue. But what you often see is the biggest corporations—Big Pharma, Big Defense, and Wall Street—lobbying at levels much, much higher than any other group, and their interests dominate our legislation. Many lobbyists even help draft and write up the bills that are presented to Congress. Do you see any conflict of interest there?

In the 1950s the proportion of government revenue brought in from corporate taxes was about 28 percent. Today, that figure is closer to 7 percent.[6] Now, I understand that many conservatives may be looking at these numbers as a win. "Low taxes! That's exactly what we want!" Yet it should be obvious when you, again, look at the size and budget of our government that they still needed to get tax dollars from somewhere to afford the bloating of the bureaucracy, and that is where *you* come in. In the 1950s, the proportion of the federal government's revenue brought in from Americans' payroll taxes was about 5.7 percent. In 2021, that number was closer to 32.5 percent.[7] What has essentially transpired is that the corporate lobbying machine has made it so now instead of their having to pay more taxes, *you* have to pay more taxes, putting the burden on normal, working-class Americans. Last time I checked, I didn't own a multi-billion-dollar corporation with access to petition the government and buy them out. Do you? Didn't think so. Sure, you can call up your congressman and gripe about the destruction of a wetland in your neighborhood that housed a protected bird species, but who are they going to listen to? You, the average Joe, or the lobbyist with hundreds of thousands, sometimes even millions of dollars drafting up a bill for him that promises him funding for his next election campaign in exchange for the destruction of the wetlands where his company's latest factory can go? You get the point. Someone please try and explain to me how the rich and powerful taking advantage of us and making themselves more rich and powerful is a sign of "democracy" or our "First Amendment at work."

Hierarchies exist. For all of human history, someone has ruled, and someone has been ruled. But that does not mean that a leader inherently has to be selfish and careless toward those underneath them. Leaders can be strong. Leaders can be good. Leaders can put the will of the people above their own when it is necessary. But when you have a ruling class that serves within a mechanism that is so easily manipulated and controlled, human nature takes its course, and despite many of our leaders' good intentions, one by one they fall to the dominion of greed, laziness, and easy decision making. The system must be changed before we expect our politicians to change, because our political apparatus works on the fact that it breeds corruption and is too easily exploited, and human nature will almost always overrule obligation.

Our politicians work on the basis of control, and it comes down to a philosophical question: If the government can take your money through taxes, why wouldn't they be able to take everything from you? If they can take 5 percent of your salary through taxes, why not 10 percent, why not 50 percent, why not 100 percent? Where is the moral line to say 5 percent is okay, yet 100 percent is not? The truth is there is no moral line, and when you give someone else even a fraction of your value, then there is no reason why they could not ordain themselves or the state to take all of it. If they can take some of your rights away, who is to say they couldn't take *all* of your rights away? It is merely a matter of subjective opinion at that point as to whether or not someone has the right to take something away from you, so the only answer is to never let them take anything away from you, because as soon as they have a morsel of your divine rights, they become the new God, able to strip away your freedoms at will based on arbitrary power that we have ceded to them.

Many people claim that the leaders of America and the West are merely totally inept. They assume that they have low intelligence and simply act and dictate in accordance with their minute brain power and their complete lack of capacity for noble ambition. But I do not think these people are stupid in the slightest. In fact, I think they see opportunity and a chance for survival, and jump to become politicians, knowing the benefits of what their new career might bring. Politics produces and attracts a certain brand of people. They sell out the first chance they get because many of them see self-preservation as the ultimate goal, not a means to be a force for positive change in a world run awry. It is the same reason why people tie themselves to political parties above all else, instead of to a higher power or the truth. Being a part of a group of others who believe as you do is much safer than being an outcast, and political parties on the Republican versus Democrat paradigm provide the perfect placement for an individual who feels they are all alone.

Auberon Herbert, a British philosopher and writer, wrote, "The great trick, the winning of power, requires ciphers, and can't be played in any other fashion. Having once turned men into ciphers, you must appeal to them as good loyal party followers…you can't appeal to them…as men, possessed of conscience, and will, and responsibility, for in that case they might once more regain possession of their suppressed consciences and their higher faculties, and begin to think and judge for themselves…The great struggle for power would die out, would come naturally to its end, when the suppression of self and the making of ciphers had ceased to be."[8] A man who thinks only along party lines ends up being totally controlled by the party, and is what Herbert describes as a cipher. A cipher is unable to think for themselves and is instead subject to the authority of what their party says is the right or wrong thing. This has contributed heavily to the massive polarization in our country. People don't see each other as people, or as children of God, they see them as members of a political party, and thus animosity is achieved solely by the fact that someone belongs to a different group than you do.

Yes, Republicans and Democrats have different platforms. Yes, I am a registered Republican and align much more heavily with the right than the left. But the disillusion creeps in when you realize that when elected, members of both parties act in similar ways, both consumed by their own self-interest. For too long, Republicans in this country have been playing the same games as the left. Republicans are just leftists driving at the speed limit, as they say. Republicans in their khaki pants partake in the same cocktail parties as the Democrats, vying for the same political donors and pushing the same policies as the left under a different name and telling you it's good for you. The masses of people controlled by the party nod their heads in approval. Most Republicans in Congress care more about what the *New York Times* writes about them than the well-being of the people they represent, just like the Democrats. Thirty members of the House and Senate from 2017 to 2019 are now lobbyists, irrelevant of political party. Half of retired U.S. senators and a third of retired U.S. House members end up back in Washington as registered lobbyists, once again, regardless of political party.[9] The parties may be different, but the people within them are exactly the same. But they know that when they turn *you* into a loyal party-over-values activist, you will fund them, you will support them, you will speak for them, and sometimes you will die for them. An eighteen-year-old boy was run over and killed by an older man in late 2022 simply because the man thought he was a Republican.[10] These are the extremes that idolatry of a political party can take you to.

The key is breaking free from the dichotomy of the two-party system. Do not vote for someone because they are a Republican. Vote for them because they are God-fearing, they promise to uphold the rule of law and the Constitution, they love the country and the people they plan to serve and lead, and they are not easily corrupted through bribes and petty vanity. Then, and only then, can we start working on the way we fix the system that broke us in the first place. Maybe we introduce a public option like some countries in Europe have, making it so that political donations cannot exceed a certain threshold for each candidate and the donations come directly from the taxpayers, not from shady PACs and secret donors. Maybe we can introduce term limits and make it so that politics isn't a lucrative career but more of an act of public service. Maybe we can ban insider trading from members of Congress who become exorbitantly wealthy betting on stocks and businesses they have a hand in promoting and growing. Maybe we can ban early voting and ballot harvesting and make elections happen only on election day, with an ID required to vote for every person. Maybe we could ban members of Congress or government from becoming lobbyists as soon as they leave office. There are many ways we can fix the predicaments our republic has gotten itself into, but it takes good people, with strong wills, who refuse to play the game. Men of real character must step forth to be more than pawns of a corporation, and men who are merely products of narcissism must be cast aside. They must put their country before themselves. They must put the people who elected them before themselves. And they must put God before themselves. I know I'm asking a lot here from our politicians, but nothing will change until the people of this country actually start asking for a lot more from the people in charge. At the end of the day, our political leaders are our employees. We "hire" them, and we pay their salaries. It is about time for them to start acting like it.

This fight is a right versus left issue—a right versus wrong issue—but it is not a Republican versus Democrat issue. If the people claiming to fight for me don't actually fight for me, they do not deserve my support. If they would rather get retweets than stop the murder of babies, they are not on my side. If they would rather get money from donors than save the middle class, they are not on my side. If they would rather sell my country overseas than stand for the Constitution, they are not on my side. We must break free from the political-party-above-all-else mindset and realize that values and ideals hold a much more noble ambition than money, tribe, and power. No longer can we play the same games as the Republican and Democrat parties, or focus on social media vanity, or cherish money above God, and expect something to change. The only way we change our world is through real, moral action, and the days of hoping someone else swoops in and saves us are over. It is about time we all take back control of our country's destiny.

Chapter 3

BIG PHARMA

No one should approach the temple of science
with the soul of a money changer.

—*Thomas Browne*

In 2021, a new movie, or should we say propaganda film, came out, titled *Mama Has a Mustache*. This film is nothing more than pro-transgender pandering, downplaying the harmful consequences of gender reassignment surgery and the psychological impacts it has on the mind of one of these confused individuals. The short film is targeted at children, the entirety of it being interviews with kids aged five to ten years old about transgenderism. The director of the film, Sally Rubin, a tenured professor at Chapman University who also proudly identifies as "queer," says she wants to get the film into classrooms and create "a teaching toolkit & discussion guide for in-classroom use."[1] This insidious film is being marketed to children and may end up in one of your child's classrooms in the near future, but what is even more disturbing is that one of the lead partners of the film is one you may not expect: Bayer, a multinational pharmaceutical company.[2]

Now, why would a multi-billion-dollar pharma company support a film like *Mama Has a Mustache*? Well, precisely for the reason you might expect. Money. Lots and lots of money. One of the drugs Bayer manufactures is a compound called cyproterone acetate, a drug for young boys to make them more feminine.[3] It is used primarily as a puberty blocker, but certain strains are also used to help men grow breasts. To me, this sure looks like Bayer is partnering with far-left causes promoting gender transitioning so they can make money off the drugs these kids take. Are they not thinking of the cost or damage done to the children who take these drugs? Please try and explain to me how Big Pharma isn't the most evil and greedy monopoly on the planet.

It has also been reported that other pharmaceutical companies, such as AbbVie Inc., sponsor such groups as the Gender Cool Project, an organization aimed at normalizing children transitioning genders.[4] AbbVie creates a drug called Lupron, another puberty-blocking drug that has also been used to castrate sex offenders.[5] As reported by Breitbart, it is also shown that many directors of various gender clinics at children's hospitals have received financial compensation from such companies as AbbVie and Endo Pharmaceuticals, both companies that, unsurprisingly, create puberty-blocking drugs that can be used on children.[6] Lupron is also an estrogen-blocking drug most commonly used in breast cancer treatment when the cancer is estrogen receptor positive. Now Lupron has a new life in the gender transition world. More profits for Big Pharma.

Why aren't our politicians speaking out about this hideous practice? Big Pharma spends more on lobbying than any other corporate sector.[7] In 2020 the pharmaceutical industry spent over $300 million lobbying the federal government. They spend almost three times as much as the oil and gas industry and almost four times as much as the education lobby. It is as Deep Throat said in *All the President's Men*: Follow the money—particularly if you are having a hard time understanding the rationale for why a pharmaceutical company would want to get behind the transgender movement.

Think about this. Big Pharma is said to spend $5.2 billion

annually on television advertising targeted primarily at the consumer.[8] It spent another $9.53 billion on digital ads aimed at consumers and corporations in just 2020 alone.[9] This consumer spending is more than *twice* what the pharmaceutical industry spends on research into new cancer drugs. As a matter of fact, nine of the ten largest American pharmaceutical companies actually spend more on *advertising* than on research and development.[10]

The United States and New Zealand are the only two countries that allow pharmaceutical companies to market straight to consumers. Yet in the case of Covid-19 vaccinations, the American companies don't really have to bother. Let's take a look at the money in the Covid-19 industrial complex.

Pfizer reported 2021 second-quarter revenues of $19 billion, and an operational growth of 86 percent. That kind of money generates plenty for a supportive marketing campaign. Here is just a partial list of where their Covid vaccine is advertised: *This Week with George Stephanopoulos, Good Morning America, Today,* CBS Sports, *Meet the Press, CBS This Morning, 60 Minutes, Anderson Cooper 360,* and *CNN Tonight.* Pfizer's global revenue doubled in 2021 to $81.3 billion, which is greater than the GDP of many countries. Pfizer expects to achieve revenues of $98 billion to $102 billion in 2022.[11]

But there is more. The U.S. government is promoting the Covid-19 vaccine more fiercely than the companies would ever probably decide to do of their own volition. According to the *Rio Times,* "The Biden administration...purchased ads in 'legacy' media publications including the *New York Post,* the *Los Angeles Times,* and *The Washington Post,* digital media companies like

BuzzFeed News and Newsmax, YouTube, and hundreds of local newspapers and TV stations."[12]

Nearly half of the funding that backs the U.S. Food and Drug Administration comes from the same industries it is mandated to watch over.[13] Do you really think the bureaucrats at the FDA are totally free to give independent opinions when these sources of money are on the line? CDC funding is similar. They also receive large grants for Covid research from the Bloomberg Family Foundation and the Bill and Melinda Gates Foundation. Imagine for a moment that the Environmental Protection Agency was heavily funded by ExxonMobil.[14] Do you see the potential for a conflict of interest in everything involving that major oil company and the EPA?

By contrast, money given to the National Institutes of Health is mostly veiled from the public. Worse, the NIH allows its publicly employed researchers to receive *royalty payments* from government-funded activities that result in private-company sales income. In addition to their taxpayer-funded bimonthly paychecks, current and former NIH researchers received yearly royalty payments averaging $9,700. Some have been reported to receive as much as $150,000 in annual royalty rewards![15]

Pause a moment. Read that last sentence again, then think about this: If I was your doctor and prescribed a medication for you and I was profiting from each prescription, could you have complete confidence in the objectivity of my recommendation?

And we can't forget the fact that the research to develop the Covid-19 vaccines was almost entirely funded by the taxpayer. Once the vaccines were developed, the distribution of the shots was further funded nearly totally by taxpayers. The record keeping and reporting on the vaccines is also at the expense of taxpayers, and the newly repurposed Pfizer drug Paxlovid, used to treat Covid, has been paid for by taxpayers.

Yet information about many of the early treatment protocols developed by private-sector doctors working on their own has been suppressed by the CDC and shunned by the FDA.[16] Drug trials were manipulated for a desired outcome.[17] Despite the helpful effects of hydrochloroquine (HCQ) in the treatment of Covid-19, the French government banned its use due to a fraudulent study published, then retracted a few days later, by *The Lancet*.[18] Another example is the RECOVERY trial, which did not show any positive effect of HCQ. In the experiment, the dose used was not only inappropriate, but may have been a disease-aggravating factor, negating the therapeutic effect.[19] Professor David Jayne of Cambridge University questions whether an intentionally high dose of HCQ was used in the RECOVERY and SOLIDARITY trials in an attempt to make the drug appear toxic.[20]

What's more is that a study found that during the Covid-19 pandemic, there was a direct connection between the money received from Gilead Sciences (the developer of remdesivir) by academic infectious diseases physicians and their public opposition to the administering of HCQ.[21] The conflicts of interest that caused the disapproval of HCQ and allowed the authorization of remdesivir runs deep, and concerns physicians, medical event organizers, publishers, and therapeutic trials. In France, Gilead Sciences is estimated to have spent $65 million over the past seven years to establish its influence with practitioners and institutions.[22]

Regardless of the fact that remdesivir has no statistically measurable clinical benefits,[23] and that it is incredibly toxic to the kidneys and lungs,[24] a 1-billion-euro contract was signed between the Gilead laboratory and the European Union.[25] Just before this contract was signed, the World Health Organization advised against the use of remdesivir because of its ineffectiveness, high renal toxicity, and high cost. There are now lawsuits being filed as a result of deaths from remdesivir.[26]

Even more depressing is that the media went along with this suppression of free speech and information. Social media companies routinely banned and deplatformed any physician or scientist speaking contrary to the bureaucratic narrative. Why? Do you think the big social media companies might also have profited from the direct-to-consumer advertising of the government-funded products in the same way as traditional media? Do you know a lot of cases where the hand that feeds is bitten?

This isn't speculation, it is big money. Consider that Pfizer expected $32 billion in Covid vaccine sales in 2022. Moderna is forecasting $19 billion in Covid sales, with the vaccine being its *only* current commercial product. Moderna had never even produced a vaccine before it developed its Covid shots. Pfizer, BioNTech, and Moderna are reported to be making $1,000 in profit every second of the business day.[27]

Big Pharma's greedy hand is not just present in our prescription and over-the-counter drugs. It is also present in our food industry. The food industry, Big Pharma, and the government agencies that oversee them do not seem to have our best interests at heart. All you need to do to verify this point is look around you to see what the overconsumption of processed, sugar-laden, highly refined foods has done.

Big Pharma has contributed to this new world of chemical engineering by providing and advertising a drug for every ailment, and many of the largest pharmaceutical companies are also in the food business as well. Could the same companies that offer cures for various diseases be contributing to the explosion of the diseases we now face? Are they profiting from both sides? That would be like owning both the local liquor store and the alcohol rehab center next door. For example, one of the largest pharmaceutical companies—Abbott Laboratories—also owns the best-selling baby formula, Similac, and is the fourth-largest manufacturer of all infant formula.

By any chance, have you reviewed the list of ingredients for Similac Sensitive infant formula? The list might shake you:

CORN SYRUP, MILK PROTEIN ISOLATE, HIGH OLEIC SAFFLOWER OIL, SUGAR, SOY OIL, COCONUT OIL; LESS THAN 2% OF: C. COHNII OIL, M. ALPINA OIL, SHORT-CHAIN FRUCTO-OLIGOSACCHARIDES, BETA-CAROTENE, LUTEIN, POTASSIUM CHLORIDE, SODIUM CITRATE, CALCIUM PHOSPHATE, POTASSIUM CITRATE, SOY LECITHIN, MAGNESIUM PHOSPHATE, CHOLINE CHLORIDE, ASCORBIC ACID, INOSITOL, ASCORBYL PALMITATE, FERROUS SULFATE, TAURINE, CALCIUM CARBONATE, CHOLINE BITARTRATE, ZINC

SULFATE, L-CARNITINE, MIXED TOCOPHEROLS, NIACINAMIDE, d-ALPHA-TOCOPHERYL ACETATE, CALCIUM PANTOTHENATE, MAGNESIUM CHLORIDE, VITAMIN A PALMITATE, COPPER SULFATE, THIAMINE HYDROCHLORIDE, RIBOFLAVIN, PYRIDOXINE HYDROCHLORIDE, FOLIC ACID, POTASSIUM IODIDE, MANGANESE SULFATE, PHYLLOQUINONE, BIOTIN, SODIUM SELENATE, VITAMIN D3, VITAMIN B12, POTASSIUM HYDROXIDE, AND NUCLEOTIDES (ADENOSINE 5'-MONOPHOSPHATE, CYTIDINE 5'-MONOPHOSPHATE, DISODIUM GUANOSINE 5'-MONOPHOSPHATE, DISODIUM URIDINE 5'-MONOPHOSPHATE).[28]

Some of the top ingredients are safflower oil, soy oil, and sugar. Many health experts now believe that vegetable and seed oils are unhealthy and inflammatory.[29] What are these inflammatory substances doing to the insides of our babies? What are their long-term consequences? And, most important, why is Big Pharma pushing these unhealthy products? Unhealthy kids and adults are ripe customers for the pharma industry's cures for the diseases and inflammatory conditions they helped usher in.

The total number of those diagnosed with cancer in the United States is growing. Estimates from Pricewaterhouse Coopers show that the number of cancer patients in the United States continues to swell, to about 18 million—up 31 percent over 2010. This despite massive R&D dollars going into cancer research. Compound this with the fact that cancer actually consists of hundreds of different diseases, giving the industry a wide array of oncological indications to target. According to the American Association for Cancer Research, the number of cancer survivors in the United States increased by 1.4 million to 16.9 million in January 2019. Speculation as to why cancer numbers are increasing is varied, but one has to consider the exposure to unhealthy foods, toxic environmental chemicals, and pollutants. If breastfeeding is healthier—and most everyone agrees with this premise—then why do we allow pharmaceutical companies to advertise and promote the unhealthier formula alternative? Why do so many maternity wards push formula feeding and give new moms formula samples? The influence of Big Pharma is not limited to the halls of Congress.

Big Pharma's influence continues to grow. It routinely forges partnerships and pours money into medical schools across our country, blurring the boundaries between for-profit companies and academic institutions. Pfizer Inc., AstraZeneca PLC, and Eli Lilly and Company are some of the largest international pharmaceutical companies signing deals with medical colleges at New York University, Harvard, and the University of California at San Francisco.[30] Big Pharma routinely sponsors drug lunches for medical students and residents, it pays stipends for professors to speak on behalf of its products, and it even funds laboratories on medical school campuses. The University of California at San Diego, Boston University, Harvard, Tufts, the University of Massachusetts, and seven academic medical centers in New York City have ventured into similar research partnerships with Pfizer. In Canada, Big Pharma even buys textbooks and supplies.[31]

Purdue Pharma, the manufacturer of OxyContin, once told physicians across the world that their product was safe, effective, and non-addicting.[32] After many years of lawsuits, Purdue Pharma has been dissolved and billions in payments have been rendered.[33] Similar practices continue today, not just with naïve and willing medical students and residents but also in medical offices and hospitals across our country. Which company and product will be the next Purdue Pharma? Approximately 90 percent of clinical drug trials reported in the major medical journals are conducted or sponsored by companies that look to benefit from the results of the studies.[34] In 2004, Richard Horton, editor of one of the most prestigious medical journals in the world, *The Lancet*, said that "journals have devolved into information laundering operations for the pharmaceutical industry."[35] In 2005, Richard Smith, former editor of the *British Journal of Medicine*, said that medical journals are an extension of the marketing arm of the big pharmaceutical companies. Furthermore, in 2005, Marcia Angell, the former editor of the *New England Journal of Medicine*, criticized the industry for becoming primarily a marketing machine. Are the big pharmaceutical companies swaying the prescribing habits of doctors?

If Big Pharma reps do not influence, then why are they paid to come into doctors' offices, hospitals, and medical schools across our country? We once allowed the tobacco industry to give out free samples of their products. They too told us their products were safe and healthy. In the 1950s, to avoid financial collapse due to the scientific link between tobacco and lung cancer, the tobacco industry created a scientific concept called "scientific uncertainty."[36] The fostering of scientific doubt allowed the industry to shift the risk to individuals and away from the company. Later, pharmaceutical companies would follow the tobacco road map. Perhaps it's time to stop the practice of pharma sponsorship throughout our health care, government, and media.

Seventy percent of Americans take at least one supplement daily, and 30 percent of adults age sixty-five and older are taking four or more supplements of any kind.[37] The supplement industry has grown to an over $28 billion market in part because 90 percent of Americans suffer from some form of vitamin deficiency. The reasons for these deficiencies are varied, but they include poor nutrition, environmental toxins, and nutrient-deficient foods. That's great news for Big Pharma, as, unlike the prescription drug industry, the supplement industry is largely unregulated.

The proposed Durbin-Braun legislation would require pre-market approval for all dietary supplements. It would mandate supplements, which are classified as foods, to go through a similar process for approval as drugs.[38] Few supplement makers have the financial resources to meet this requirement, and if enacted it would put many of them out of business. For years the FDA and the pharmaceutical industry have tried to get supplements off the market. Another strategy is for Big Pharma companies to purchase supplement brands. Just fourteen mega-corporations, many of them drug companies, own more than a hundred of the most popular supplement brands on the market. Owning the majority of supplement companies places the drug industry in a position where they are able to get rid of them whenever they want to or just increase prices. This monopoly over the supplement industry also gives drug companies enormous regulatory power and influence. The Durbin-Braun legislation would further that monopoly.

A recent example of this was during the early part of the Covid pandemic in 2020 when the FDA tried to ban the supplement N-acetylcysteine (NAC). NAC has been used widely for decades as a supplement. Specifically, many health care practitioners recommend it to help with Covid-related fatigue and as an antioxidant. There are more than a thousand NAC-containing products on the market. Amazon for a while stopped allowing the sale of NAC-containing products—but this has since been reversed. The arguments by the FDA and others are that because of the low level of regulation of the supplement industry, the public is at risk due to unsafe products. As a short reminder, the companies that make childhood vaccines are immune from all liability if someone is injured by their jab. Nutritional supplements are some of the safest food products available. Deaths associated with dietary supplements are extremely rare compared to prescriptions or even over-the-counter drugs.[39] For example, Tylenol or the generic acetaminophen is "responsible for 56,000 emergency department visits, 2,600 hospitalizations, and 500 deaths per year in the United States," according to one study, which adds that 51 percent of these incidents are "unintentional overdoses."[40] From March 2021 to March 2022, according to the CDC, more than 109,000 people died due to overdosing on drugs.[41]

The supplement industry is growing rapidly and is a threat to Big Pharma as more people are becoming skeptical of the health care industry and are taking responsibility for their own health. In addition, more and more people are looking to alternative health providers such as naturopaths and chiropractors to get help. These alternative health providers often rely on supplements and nutraceuticals to help patients, and compared to MDs, they use many fewer prescription drugs.

A Gallup poll from 2019 found that the pharmaceutical sector is the most loathed industry in the country. It scored a net favorability rating of minus-31 points—that is, 27 percent positive and 58 percent negative.[42] There are many reasons for this, and some are justified. The perception by much of the public is that Big Pharma cares more about profits than people. It is easy to understand this sentiment when the cost of prescription drugs is increasing by roughly 10 percent every year.[43] This means they double in price every seven years. Several recent examples of what seemed to be price gouging have left a bad taste in the minds of consumers. When the Mylan pharmaceutical company raised the price of an EpiPen to levels never seen before, it was hard to believe it was anything but price gouging on this lifesaving drug for severe allergic reactions. A lawsuit ensued, and preliminary approval from a federal judge in Kansas was given for a $264 million settlement with affiliates of Mylan NV.[44] There are multiple other examples of similar practices, including with the lifesaving drug Daraprim. Martin Shkreli—you may have seen his smirking face on TV—was sentenced to seven years for securities fraud. Shkreli pushed up the price of Daraprim, a drug that is primarily used as a treatment for AIDS patients or those with weakened immune systems. It was originally marked at $13.50, yet in typical greedy Big Pharma fashion, Shkreli raised the price of the lifesaving drug to $750, close to fifty-six times the original cost.[45]

Patent law shenanigans have also led to the unfavorable reputation of the pharmaceutical industry.[46] The federal government incentivizes innovation by providing drug companies with patents that prevent competition so that they may recoup their R&D costs and make a profit. However, many of these companies play games with the patent process, trying to extend the patents or adding to their chemicals prior to the patent expiration in order to extend the patent. The company AbbVie, for example, was sued for erecting a "patent thicket" comprising over a hundred patents to protect its drug Humira (the best-selling drug in the world at the time) from generic competition.[47] Allergan attempted to skirt the system by transferring one of its patents to an Indian tribe.[48] This effort was eventually stopped by the Supreme Court.

Another reason why the pharmaceutical industry is disliked is due to a recent FDA initiative. In 2019, the FDA released a list of Big Pharma companies that could be seen as knowingly obstructing their rivals from breaking into the drug industry.

By showcasing what Big Pharma is doing, we can potentially shame them into good behavior with the help of public opinion to curb some of their nefarious practices.[49] We have to hold these people accountable.

From capitalizing on the era of gender transition to the insidious relationship of Big Pharma with the government during Covid, to the price-gouging practices of some companies, the pharmaceutical industry has earned its reputation. Pharmaceutical products play an important role in our society, and many lifesaving products have improved the lives of millions. However, it is critical that the public be aware of some of the less desirable practices that often occur and are allowed by government involvement and corrupt incentives. The solution is not larger government involvement or even more regulation but rather more transparency and public involvement in ensuring that public interests, not profits, are put first. So the next time your doctor prescribes you that new "lifesaving" medicine, try to remember who might be profiting off of you getting it.

This chapter was written with the help of Dr. Jeff Barke.

Chapter 4

BIG TECH

The permanent lie becomes the only safe form of existence...Every wag of the tongue can be overheard by someone, every facial expression observed by someone. Therefore every word, if it does not have to be a direct lie, is nonetheless obliged not to contradict the general, common lie. There exists a collection of ready-made phrases, of labels, a selection of ready-made lies.

—Aleksandr Solzhenitsyn

Big tech companies made $1.4 trillion during the pandemic.[1] As people stayed home out of fear of the virus and consumed themselves with social media and online shopping, Big Tech made record high profits off people's new habits. Should it be any surprise then that the big tech companies would want to stifle the truth about the true nature of COVID, its origins, and how deadly it actually was, when if the reality of the situation came out, it would send people off their phones and back to work? I don't think so. Big Tech profits off people's hard times and the destructive aspects of our human nature, and leeches off people it knows it can take advantage of for profits and agenda.

Social media is the reason I was able to get the job I have in the first place—there is no denying that. Being able to post videos on Instagram and Facebook for the world to see and to publish my opinions on Twitter is how I was able to achieve the success I have accomplished. Social media is the reason why I became a national bestselling author for my first book, and the reason why I was able to drop out of school to write, speak around the world, become editor in chief of a newspaper, produce documentaries, and make hundreds of videos amassing over a billion views since I got started about six years ago. Due to all this, I understand the benefits and usefulness of what social media can do, and I will not belittle every part of it as useless or evil. I think people can use certain aspects of it for degrees of varying good and purposes, but I also think there is a deep malice behind the people in charge of these platforms that makes them so easy to abuse.

In late 2022, Elon Musk purchased Twitter, to the shock of many. I, for one, was convinced the deal would never go through, and then when it did, I was ecstatic. Things were about to change on the platform. Although there was still the banning of accounts, and shadow banning and silencing of many dissenting voices, many accounts were reinstated that had been previously removed, and it seemed like many tweets that used to get a warning label on them were now free to exist without a label of misinformation. But the best part of Elon Musk's purchase of Twitter was the release of the Twitter files—documents and communications from Twitter executives prior to Musk's purchase that he turned over to journalists. These showed the true deviance and malpractice the company was engaging in.

To fully understand how much power these big tech companies have, you have to look no further than the banning of our then sitting president, Donald Trump, on Twitter. Trump used Twitter as a means to communicate with his constituents when he was president, as a platform to discuss policies, give the country updates on the state of America, and keep the public informed. Yes, he did the occasional Twitter trolling as well, but that is not why he was removed from the platform. Despite his breaking no violations, his banning seemed to be solely for political reasons, which sets a massive precedent for the lengths that these social media companies are willing to go to for their agenda. Not even the sitting president of the United States is safe from the ban hammer if their politics don't follow the "right message," and that is truly a frightening thought. After January 6, 2021, and the events that took place at the U.S. Capitol, Yoel Roth, the "trust and safety" chief at Twitter, met with the FBI and the Department of Homeland Security.[2] None of these meetings or what transpired in them were made available to the public. But it gets much worse than that when you dig into the Twitter files more and see what was really happening behind the scenes.

The first release of these files took place on December 2, 2022. They detailed what was going on in Twitter's headquarters in the closing days of the 2020 election when the company restricted the *New York Post* story igniting the Hunter Biden laptop scandal. To the public, the story was blocked by Twitter because it was based on "hacked materials." Yet documents show that executives at the company knew there were going to be issues with this decision due to the fact that the *New York Post* was not the entity that hacked the documents in the story and this was taking place during a presidential campaign.[3] But this didn't stop Twitter from going through with their censorship anyway. December 8 is when things really started to heat up, when Musk released new documents to former *New York Times* reporter Bari Weiss to report on.[4] These latest revelations from Weiss showed Twitter's secret blacklists and proof that they were in fact shadow banning people, although they called it "visibility filtering." One Twitter employee was quoted as saying, "Think about visibility filtering as being a way for us to suppress what people see to different levels. It's a very powerful tool." These files showed how different accounts were being actively shadow banned on the platform, as well as not amplified, as in conservative thought leader Charlie Kirk's case, among others, and put on "search blacklists." Turns out all those "conspiracy theories" conservatives had about social media censorship were true.

Part 6 of the Twitter files revealed that the FBI was working hand in hand with Twitter and was frequently sending reports to the company. Twitter received moderation requests from the FBI, Homeland Security, and other government agencies about accounts and classified information.[5] It was even revealed that Twitter received compensation for "processing requests" from the FBI, which spent millions of dollars to censor information from the public.[6] In part 8, it was revealed that Twitter actively knew about and was supporting Pentagon-backed covert operations. Part 10 revealed how the Biden administration worked with Twitter on silencing and banning accounts when it came to the Covid-19 debate. The Biden admin was "very angry" that more accounts pushing what they deemed as misinformation weren't banned, and expressed this in memos to Twitter staff.[7] These files showed that the Biden team had a direct line to executives at Twitter to censor tweets. In part 12, it was revealed that Twitter took private requests from government agencies and officials, such as Congressman Adam Schiff, for content moderation and the banning of accounts.

I read all of this and thought, *What the actual hell is wrong with these people?* There is now definitive proof that Twitter censored people on their platform when they said they were not, proof that they worked hand in hand with our own government to shut people down, proof that they were compensated by the government for doing so, and proof that the Biden administration knew all of this was going on and even made special requests. This just makes you think: If this is what has been exposed so far, what else are they doing behind closed doors? And what are other tech companies that are even bigger and wealthier than Twitter doing in unison with our government to silence us?

Yet as damning as all of this is, I have very little faith that anything will be done about it. I am writing this chapter of this book in January 2023, and by the time this book comes out I am almost certain no politician will step up to do anything about it. You think Biden will do something about it? He was part of it! You think the Republican Party will do anything about it? Politicians on both sides of the aisle take money from Big Tech for their campaigns, and they aren't about to lose that paycheck. They may talk a big game about doing something and say they want to "protect your free speech," but none of them have ever put their money where their mouth is. Trump was president for four years and did nothing of real consequence to curb social media censorship or put a halt to the monopoly they built. If he couldn't, or wouldn't, do anything about this issue, what makes you think anyone else will? Especially when you have so many different government agencies working hand in hand with big tech companies. I am sure there will be some lawsuits, such as Alex Berenson and his lawsuit suing Twitter over his account suspension, but these will only be a drop in the bucket compared to the real power Big Tech has, and will not stop their steady growth, power, and the dominance they have over the American people.

So what do we do? I'd love to say that there are great alternatives to the big companies for connecting with others, say Gettr, Gab, or Parler, but let's be realistic here. I love Gettr and still post all the videos I make on there, but its slice of the market share is not competing with Twitter, TikTok, or Instagram. None of them are. It is not that these are bad applications or bad services; they just aren't what people know, so people don't want to switch. Many of these platforms as well host mostly conservatives, and to me that is not conducive to what a broad social media platform is supposed to look like. Sure, if you want to make this a forum for just conservatives to speak freely and converse among themselves, then you have that, but if you are trying to create a true rival to the big boys, it is not going to work. Especially when you disregard the biggest draw of social media for the majority of people: visibility to the opposite sex.

People, especially the younger generation, use social media as a means to present themselves as an attractive partner. It may sound Freudian to say, but social media is a conduit for dating, validation through imagery, and sexual activity. Many people might not even know it, but just look at the founding of Facebook and its inception through FaceMash, the original website Mark Zuckerberg made, where people would go online and rate the looks of girls they knew at Harvard. That is what gave Zuckerberg the idea for Facebook. It was a way for people in college to see who their classmates were dating and look at pictures of each other.[8] Social media today is a way for men and women to present themselves to the world and showcase what makes them "unique" and alluring. I am not saying that a Gettr or Parler need to institute these types of elements into their service or that it is the right thing to do, but if they ever want to be a true competitor to the massive social media companies, this is how they would have to do it. My pastor, who used to be a college pastor, always talks about how the reason why so many young men came to his youth sermons: because they knew there would be girls there to meet. Except after he was done preaching, the students could actually meet each other in person, not just like pictures of the opposite sex on Instagram. But this ease of seeing possible sexual partners from an app on your phone without putting in any effort has led to a vexing problem: the accessibility of porn.

The people in charge of these apps know exactly what they are doing. Don't think for even a second they aren't aware of the tactics they use to keep people inundated with their platforms. If you go on Instagram and TikTok, you will see what is practically porn all over the app. It isn't explicit sex scenes per se, but about as close as you can get without showing full-on nudity. It is highly sexualized videos and pictures, especially in the reels section on Instagram. Once you've seen one of these types of videos, Instagram pushes more and more similar content to you nonstop on your explore page and suggested videos, and there is no way for you to control what is on that page. Instagram pushes what can only be described as softcore porn to people who go on their app, an app used by children and impressionable young men who become addicted to the visuals of attractive and sexualized women at their fingertips any time of day. This is just one of the many ways they get people hooked. They don't want you to go out and meet people, they want you to direct message people and watch the free porn readily available at any time. It destroys human interaction, turns women into sexual objects to be gawked at and men into addicted consumers. It is all a part of the brave new world, keeping you distracted and entertained, away from the true value of life.

As you will see later in this book, I have no problem with division, and believe it can be useful for separating yourself from evil. You should not be joining forces with evil and immoral entities and should instead seek to defeat them and bring about goodness. But the faux division created by big tech platforms between people is only a conduit toward hate and unnecessary vitriol, and these companies fuel this through their algorithms and content. If you constantly like content from Fox News and *The Daily Wire*, more conservative content will be fed to you. If you are more of a CNN and *New York Times* enjoyer, then more left-wing content will be presented on your feed. It is merely a matter of the algorithm showing content to you that they believe will keep you on the application longer, thus seeing more ads, thus making them more money. The big tech companies have no issue with stoking political division, because it gives them business and makes you a consumer.

With all that being said, do you think it may be the case, then, that many political issues we discuss online are merely embellishments and dramatizations that serve the purpose of dividing us for meaningless "political" reasons? This is all according to the plans of the elite. They keep you distracted with nonsense politics, teach you to hate your fellow man, and make you think it is Republicans versus Democrats instead of all of us versus the elites that are in control. People will always talk about conservative censorship on big tech platforms, but I never see conservatives getting censored for the benign political issues of the day, or for lukewarm takes that are posted solely to fire someone up on the other side. The ideas that are censored are almost always the issues that expose the corruption of the elite. Think Covid vaccines, the lockdowns, the Ukraine agenda, the 2020 election, or the truth about climate change. These are the ideas that get censored, because they expose the oligarchy's plans, not the conservative talking points about the minimum wage or feminism. In fact, most normal conservative issues and takes are indeed quite popular, and the only reason why everyone and their mom can now have a podcast and be a "conservative influencer" or talking head is because these base takes are totally accepted by the people who run the big tech companies. They want people to engage in these types of political discussions and hate someone else who doesn't think exactly like them. They want you to mindlessly and fruitlessly debate for hours on end in comment sections. This all drives business and makes the people easier to control. The masses are so worried about arguments online with someone they have never met on meaningless political issues that they never take the time to ponder the real truths that are being orchestrated by the elites behind the scenes. Distractions, distractions, distractions...

So big tech companies profit off our tragedies, pay politicians on both sides of the aisle, censor the truth, divide us on meaningless grounds, and inundate us with hypersexualized content while keeping us addicted to their platforms through cheap dopamine hits. Sounds pretty bleak. As of this writing, big tech platforms are able to act as a publishing tool with editorial control as well as a public forum open to all. They get to have their cake and eat it too, getting tax breaks from the government for their alleged "virtue" of being free and neutral entities. But we all know that is not the case.

Section 230 of the Communications Decency Act, established roughly twenty-five years ago, essentially holds these digital companies not liable for the content that is put on their platform. The repealing of Section 230 would mean an entity like Facebook would now be responsible as the editor and publisher for all of the speech that takes place on its site, opening it up to millions upon millions of cases of libel and defamation.[9] But just repealing Section 230 is not a solution for our big tech ills, and it would completely neuter what social media is and would make posting rules even more stringent. It could possibly be amended, but with all of the voices involved, this sounds like a bureaucratic, political, legal, and financial nightmare for the American people, and would probably only result in a deal being made that grants special favors to some and benefits the elite regardless.

So what can be done? Well, as the title of this book suggests, do not comply. Do not comply with the notion that you must be a social media addict. We must take responsibility for our own agency and not expect some politician to change the rules or some altruistic CEO to make sweeping reforms. If we have issues with social media platforms, stop going on them, or at least limit yourself. If you don't like the fact that TikTok is a national security risk as a Chinese-owned company that is selling your data to the CCP, then don't use TikTok. I truly wish there was some grand solution to make all these problems go away, but I see it more as a matter of personal strength and willpower over government intervention, at least for the foreseeable future. Of course, you can't escape it all as your phone tracks your location and Google sees all your habits whether you like it or not, but what I can tell you is that every person I have talked to who has deleted their social media accounts, or at least taken breaks, is much happier than the people who spend all their time on these apps. Even simple changes such as not waking up and immediately shocking your brain by going on your phone, and instead taking a walk or making some coffee, can have significant impacts on your mental health. My generation is the most anxious, lonely, and depressed we have seen in a very long time, and it shouldn't be perplexing to ascertain the reason for it when you see them always comparing themselves to others on social media.

We can't fix the Silicon Valley world all by ourselves, but we can help ourselves. Stop letting the elites divide and conquer us on the basis of distractions. Stop letting them control all of the information and seek out truth without their help. And stop letting them dominate your mind and purpose. This might all sound more philosophical and metaphysical than some concrete government policy decision, but at the end of the day, as with most things, much of it comes down to personal responsibility and ownership of our own lives and what we surround ourselves with. If we all start to admonish these companies through our will of choosing not to partake in their psychological operations and control, then there is no doubt that one day their power will falter. Remember, they need us, we don't need them.

Chapter 5

BIG MEDIA

It was a fatal day when the public discovered that
the pen is mightier than the paving-stone, and can
be made as offensive as the brickbat. They at once
sought for the journalist, found him, developed him,
and made him their industrious and well-paid servant.
It is greatly to be regretted, for both their sakes.

—Oscar Wilde

Often when I talk to people about the media landscape, I hear a lot of blame on both sides. The left will claim Fox News and other conservative media have brainwashed our grandparents and serve only to divide us, whereas the right will claim the mainstream media is fake news and controlled by the elite agenda. But no matter who you ask, almost everyone will say that there is a big problem with the media on either side. And that problem is that they do not serve the people, and do not profess the truth. As the editor in chief of *The Florida Standard*, my Florida-based online newspaper, I am all too accustomed to attacks on media bias and credibility. No matter what we post, there is always some guy in our replies on Twitter claiming we are propaganda, or that we have shady funding, or that we are puppets, or my favorite, that I am ugly and stupid. But can you blame them for these attacks? (Well, maybe the ugly and stupid one. Even *Rolling Stone* calls me handsome in their hit pieces on me, but the others not so much.)[1] The media has betrayed the American people and turned their back on integrity in favor of serving whoever funds their operation, so the fact that we are a casualty of this vitriol is completely justified to me. When people feel they have been stabbed in the back by the media over and over, they find it very hard to trust again.

Many people think this is some new issue, that just recently the media has turned coats and switched to the side of the elite instead of the modern-day plebeians, yet the historical record paints a different picture. The largest media and news organizations have always served the elite and kept the powerful in good standing through the fear and shame of the citizens. In 1938, Hitler was named *Time*'s Man of the Year, which *Time* said they bestowed on him due to his impact on history that year, yet I doubt it is an accolade many would agree he deserved.[2] That is a common example many of you have probably heard, but what was the *New York Times* doing during all this? Well, instead of using their platform to showcase the evils of Nazi Germany, the *New York Times Magazine* was busy reporting on Hitler's mountain chalet and what took place there.[3] This wasn't an accident, either. It was published six years after the first concentration camp was opened in Dachau, nine months after the violent anti-Jewish pogroms of Kristallnacht, and just twelve days before Germany would invade Poland. The *Times* even went so far to say that Hitler's study created "an atmosphere of quiet cheerfulness." And the *New York Times* wasn't the only one writing fluff pieces about Hitler.

The *New York Times*'s bad track record doesn't stop there, though, and what is worse, it was handsomely rewarded with a Pulitzer Prize in the 1930s despite apparent lies and false reporting in the heralded stories. In 1932, Walter Duranty won a Pulitzer Prize for his reporting on communism and Stalin in the Soviet Union—the term "reporting" is used lightly here. The *Times* has even received calls to return the award for Duranty's work. His work was more akin to a cover-up of atrocities committed by the communists, and instead of being chastised for his lies and Marxist sympathies, he was rewarded with awards and fame. He received exclusive interviews with Stalin, and claimed Stalin was the strong leader that Russia needed. One of the articles cited in his win of the Pulitzer led with: "Russia today cannot be judged by Western standards or interpreted in Western terms." Anyone who knows history will know that Stalin's actions led to the deaths of millions of people, and that communism in the Soviet Union was a great evil that brought only torment and despair. Yet Duranty in all his reporting omitted these facts, using words like "malnutrition" instead of starvation, and claiming that crop harvests were definitive proof that there was no famine like other journalists claimed.[4]

You have to remember that at this time there was no social media, and there were no videos coming out of the Soviet Union on people's phones to show what was really transpiring. All we had really was the word of journalists like Duranty, and their reporting shaped public decision making and attitudes toward foreign places that others couldn't get to or experience firsthand. Walter Duranty and the *New York Times* probably knew this and used it to manipulate an American population to sympathize with communism, an ideology that killed more people than the Nazis and that some countries are still recovering from to this day. This is the real power of the media.

Power comes from the majority, and six corporations control roughly 90 percent of the media landscape: General Electric, Disney, Viacom, News Corp, Time Warner, and Columbia Broadcasting System (CBS).[5] That means that roughly 230 media executives control the media and information supply of hundreds of millions of Americans. Many of the most popular news outlets and media companies are owned by these big six, such as ESPN, Marvel, the *Wall Street Journal*, Comcast, *Time*, CNN, and Fox. Do you see the conflict of interest that could arise here with the most powerful and wealthiest men in the world owning the majority of the media in the West? It means that they decide what runs and what doesn't, and most of the time if it doesn't benefit them, their stakeholders, their wallets, and their plays for power, then it doesn't run.

Think about Jeff Bezos, the third-richest person in the world and founder and executive chairman of Amazon, who owns the *Washington Post*. He once considered buying CNN, according to anonymous bankers. Amazon has an annual lobbying budget of $20 million, and is one of the top dogs when it comes to spending money in Washington, D.C.[6] It has used this cash to fight internet regulations, tax policy, labor laws, antitrust issues, and more. So if Amazon is willing to spend this amount of money lobbying the government, setting aside the interests of its workers and the American taxpayer for its own gain, what do you think it would be willing to do with the media companies it outright owns? There is no doubt that much of the reporting that the *Washington Post* carries out is influenced by the financial and power interests of Bezos. For another example, take *Vox*, the popular news outlet. In June 2021, it published an article titled "Wall Street Isn't to Blame for the Chaotic Housing Market," essentially absolving BlackRock and the rest of Wall Street of all guilt for their purchasing of single-family homes across America and turning them into rental properties.[7] A hedge fund like BlackRock (which we will get into in the next chapter) pushes heavily for ESG standards and "anti-racist" principles in business, yet then buys single-family homes and turns them into rentals. If you wanted to be anti-racist, you wouldn't take away minorities' best way to build wealth in

America, which is purchasing a home, and make this a nation of renters! The key about this article is that *Vox* can use whatever fancy, persuasive language and statistics in their articles that they want. But it seems far more likely that this article was created solely because Comcast has a large financial backing in *Vox*, investing $200 million in their parent company, Vox Media Inc.[8] And guess who owns a large share of Comcast? You guessed it: BlackRock. It also doesn't help that the CEO of a *Vox* investor, General Atlantic, is also on the board of BlackRock, but this could really go on for days.[9] You could look at any of the major media platforms in this country today and come to the same conclusion with all of them: The articles they write and the stories they produce aren't so much journalistic works of merit or investigation but merely empty husks of what a story is supposed to be, and nothing more than print on a screen whose words are sold to the highest bidder.

So what do you get when a small group of people has such dominance over most newspapers, radio, TV shows, and all other forms of media and entertainment? You get mass control. Narratives can be decided among them, and the current message of the day that the elites want to be pushed can be coordinated accordingly to all sorts of different channels and outlets. Media is a monopoly in America and throughout the West, and the biggest conglomerates control the information and entertainment being pushed to the majority of people.

Imagine for a moment you were born on an island, with no access to the outside world. You could get no news, media, or information from anything but your surroundings, except for one TV that only plays CNN. Yes, this might sound like a nightmare to a lot of you, but just try to think about how that would affect you. With CNN being your only option for news of the world, you are bound to believe the news presented on that channel. In our world today, with so much of the media controlled with the same stories and opinions as every other, people essentially become this person marooned on an island. Sure, you may be able to choose MSNBC over CNN, or the *Washington Post* over the *New York Times*, or Fox over Newsmax, but in the end it all boils down to mostly the same opinions and the same coverage from any source you choose. The illusion of choice is once again present here, and is cleverly used to give you, the consumer, a false sense that the gravitas of your media consumption is "unique" and "special," when in reality it is quite similar to everybody else's.

A mass media narrative is useful for one reason in particular for the elites: fear. Fear is powerful, and fear is control. Fear turns the most sensible man into a slave. A man who is afraid will perform any directions given him, and will discard his convictions for a remedy of safety. He ceases to be his own man for appeasement of danger, and instead transforms into a follower of the so-called tragedy savior. Fear of isolation, fear of shame, fear of safety: All forms of fear serve the design of the oligarchy. Once the people are afraid, they are the elite's possession to be molded and led, ripe to be marshaled into the "safety" that only those on top can provide. The great irony is that those who claim they are the salvation for the fear you hold are usually the same ones who stoked the fear in the first place.

Let's look at a more modern example. KFOR, an NBC affiliate out of Oklahoma, published a story claiming gunshot victims and people with other serious injuries were being turned away from local emergency rooms. They wrote this according to a quote from *one* doctor, who claimed this was happening because the hospital was inundated with people who had overdosed on ivermectin.[10] Think about this for a moment. It would have taken just one call to one of these local hospitals to disprove this claim, yet KFOR didn't even do that. They ran the story regardless. The hospital system this story was referring to even claimed afterward that they had not treated even one case of an ivermectin overdose. This is what qualifies for journalism these days. Whenever I have my journalists write any story, I always make sure they request comments from both sides of the story, otherwise it is incomplete. Even if one side doesn't respond, you can at least say you tried to hear their side of the story. This is what we call journalistic integrity. But it seems that the leftist-dominated media of today has none. Just using ivermectin as an example again, think of the countless articles and news stories that came out calling the drug a "horse dewormer" and claiming it was going to irreparably damage you. Ivermectin is as benign a drug as they come, yet the media ran with the lies that it would kill you, and because of this, many people missed out on a medicine that could have saved their lives, either because they believed all the falsehoods, or because their pharmacists wouldn't prescribe it for ideological reasons. What an absolutely backwards world we live in.

In 2021, when I used to live in Los Angeles, my girlfriend at the time and I took my dog Rocky to the dog park, and he frolicked around, joyfully chasing all the other dogs. As he played, we got into a conversation with a man who started talking about his job and family and eventually about how crazy the world was with Covid. I told him I just recently had it, he asked if I was okay, and I said yes, I had taken ivermectin and hydroxychloroquine. The man stared at me aghast, shook his head, called me a "f——ing psychopath," and got his dog and left. My girlfriend and I looked at each other and then started laughing hysterically. It was probably for the best: Rocky didn't like his Chihuahua anyway.

This is the power of media lies. A seemingly normal man with a normal job, family, and social life who was not some brain-dead person had been completely smothered by fake truths invented by the media and their higher-ups to then got enough of an ego to climb on his all-knowing moral pedestal and call me a psychopath for taking a drug that has been used for years on all sorts of patients around the world. And this is just one example. When you see the derangement that someone can face from just one story, imagine what a network of TV, movies, pop culture, newspapers, social media, magazines, podcasts, advertisements, "studies," press conferences, and sports can do to someone's ability to think for themselves and their inevitable brainwashing. In all honesty, I find it hard to blame the people who have become nothing more than puppets of the establishment, because of how constantly inundated people can be with the media world around them. I feel sorry for them for their brainwashing, and I feel sad and ashamed that we have a media that so actively works to deceive the very people who are supposed to trust them.

The mainstream media is nothing more than a mechanism for mass formation psychosis. As Nietzsche said, "Just see these superfluous ones! Sick are they always; they vomit their bile and call it a newspaper. They devour one another and cannot even digest themselves." And he is correct, it really is word vomit. The media is a mechanism used by the elites, along with drugs, social media, vapid cultural norms, and nonsense political debate, to keep you doped up and content with their rules and standards. Running a news organization myself, I cannot tell you how easy it is to fall into the trap of creating just the content people want to see yet maybe don't need to see. I have been in the political world long enough to know the takes and issues that get clicks solely based on shock factor alone, and which ones don't. If you post enough videos and write enough articles you end up knowing which ones will be viral, which ones will cause controversy, and which ones will flop. Everyone else with a successful media business knows these unwritten standards as well, and many fall into the trap of trying to appease customers with spectacle and flash instead of information and real news. At the end of the day they are a business and are trying to turn a profit, which I understand, so don't take this as me coming and saying no article or news hit should ever be sexy or interesting. What I am saying is that the media has lost its integrity, and instead of supplementing a potential viral story with good sources, fact checking, and interviews on both sides, it is now just a race to see who can get the story out the fastest and up on Twitter, sacrificing all elements of research that should really go into a story for quick social media likes and virality. When newspapers were daily or when nightly news shows had more time to prepare, journalists would take their time with a piece and qualify the statements they would write or present with facts and research. In the instant news world we live in today, journalists and news stations must now choose to either present a well-researched story, or be the first to report on it. Almost everyone chooses the second.

Our media world has become almost entirely reactionary. Early this year while writing this book, I had a girl call me and ask why I haven't been posting as many videos as I used to. I told her that other than writing a book and being quite busy with that, I did not find that many of the issues deserved the attention they get in the social media and news landscape of today. I think both conservatives and leftists have realized that you can easily make a name for yourself these days as a "media personality" or influencer by merely copying and pasting lukewarm Republican or Democrat talking points. There is no depth. This is not me admonishing the good people out there who promote a better culture and fight valiantly against the powers that be; this is me chastising the copious numbers of people who use the media simply for their own benefit. There is no thought required to take a breaking story, embellish the drama of it in a tweet, and go viral. The political landscape today on social media seems to be nothing but reactions to events that take place from people who care more about the vanity of what their "takes" will bring them than the consequences of the events themselves.

For example, many of these conservative "influencers" want to speak on the harm being done to children by the left. A noble cause to support indeed, yet what this seems to amount to is nothing more than tweets or Instagram posts exclaiming disgust or witty remarks on whatever leftist viral video is going through the rounds that day. As soon as the tweet is posted, they have forgotten about it and are looking for the next piece of content to react to so they can once again bring the attention back to themselves. And yes, after seven years in this industry, I have become quite cynical in regard to the conservative influencer movement in general, and it's hard to find authenticity with many of the people professing "conservatism" on these platforms. And the only reason I feel like I have the right to even say any of this is because I have been just as guilty of this type of behavior as the next guy. But the first step to creating a better political environment in our new tech-dominated world is to realize the state of affairs we are in. It is why I don't make many of the reaction-type videos I used to, and try to make only the videos and posts I really believe in. I'm not trying to fault anyone who participates in this reactionary media landscape—I get it—but I am not going to praise the conservative movement and its growth because we have such a large presence on social media and so many influencers when I believe the majority of it is inauthentic. Especially when it is the elites of this country who *want* us to tap into the vanity-seeking aspects of human nature with this type of content and news and become slaves to the new gods we have fashioned ourselves into out of cheap talking points and social media likes and views. The elites are fine with you tweeting about their evil, but they aren't very keen on you actually doing something about it. Just remember that the next time you see another viral post from your favorite political voice, and think about the place it is coming from. Was it posted for you to see? Or did they just post it for themselves?

The media world needs a major upheaval. As a concerned citizen, if you want this change to take place, you first have to choose wisely where you decide to get your news from. Are you getting it from the mainstream sector that is bought and paid for, or from an alternative news source? Are you getting it from someone spreading information for their own clout, or from someone who cares deeply about the issues they present? You might not be able to bring down a Comcast or CNN by switching your dollar away from them, but you can at least make *yourself* more educated and better informed. We don't want to be reactionary media viewers. That is what the elites want from us. We need to be an informed populace that gets real news and information from trusted sources who care about integrity and holding the elites accountable for their actions. Sure, you may get labeled a nut for reading the small online paper with three journalists instead of the multinational billion-dollar media conglomerate, but that is okay. Do not be dismayed at the fact that other people will look down on your choice of media consumption. Be proud of the fact that you are doing what you can to set the media landscape right again.

Chapter 6

AMERICA'S FINANCIAL INSTITUTIONS

The Fed has become an accomplice in the support of totalitarian regimes throughout the world.

—G. Edward Griffin

The silver lining when it comes to talking about America's financial institutions is that everyone already has a negative opinion of them. Whether you are on the left or the right, or not politically affiliated at all, it seems to me in many conversations I've had that most people despise Wall Street and the massive investment firms in control of this country. This makes it easy to discuss them with any audience, but it begs the question: As an industry so widely hated and seen as so greedy and worthless, how do they still maintain so much power over people?

One of the biggest façades of our age is the prominence of so-called experts. If you can make normal people feel as though they are inexperienced, stupid, or unqualified to speak on issues, make decisions, or handle their own finances, then you can maintain power by claiming you are the authority on whatever subject you are speaking on. Tell the people they need you to make choices and think for them, and you will dominate them forever. Blast them from your ivory towers and make them feel inadequate, and you can get them to do anything. Whether it is the Covid experts, the university experts, or the financial experts, all of them have something to gain by claiming their own elite knowledge on a certain topic that you don't possess. Most of these people who claim to be experts are merely people propped up by the establishment to convey the gravitas of whatever new message needs to be pushed that day. They tell you "not to worry, the experts are handling it." They tell you "don't try and understand Wall Street and the stock market and finances, it is too difficult. Just leave your money with us and trust us that it is all being taken care of diligently and responsibly." What an absolute load of nonsense that is.

The majority of these financial experts couldn't actually tell you jack about economics. Most of the biggest firms rely so heavily on technology that it is a miracle they even still hire people. BlackRock, one of the biggest investment firms in the world, uses software called Aladdin, which is a network of over five thousand computers that monitors all markets and client investments. This highly advanced network of computers is what really gives the BlackRock guys the means to control the financial market. The "expert" moniker is merely a way to posture themselves as superior to you and keep you oblivious to all they do. It is easy to just imagine these finance men in New York and D.C. as nothing more than greedy, sex-addicted Wolf of Wall Street druggies, but their avarice goes much deeper than that, and has given these companies more power than you could even imagine.

Let's start with some history. Do you know what the Federal Reserve is? Most people have no idea at all what the Fed is, so don't feel bad if you couldn't answer the question. The Fed is the central banking system of the United States. It was created in 1913 after secret meetings took place in 1910 to discuss a new central bank and the dissolution of the money trust in the United States. Top bankers, such as members of the Rockefeller family and J. P. Morgan, and Nelson Aldrich, the Republican Senate whip at the time, attended this secret get-together. There were seven men at the meeting on Jekyll Island, Georgia, and they accounted for nearly one-quarter of the wealth in the entire world.[1] These were very powerful men. To make a long story short, these men developed the idea of the Federal Reserve based on the principles of other central banks in Europe. The Federal Reserve Act would pass Congress in 1913, and usher in the beginning of our nation's ability to turn its people into economic slaves.

Central banks have tried to make their way into America before, yet this was never fully realized until the Federal Reserve. Andrew Jackson even went so far as to end the government's use of the Second Bank of the United States, the country's national bank, withdrawing all federal funds from the bank. Jackson did not like that it seemed as if the bank unfairly represented the political and financial interests of wealthy businessmen and oppressed the common man. Jackson truly was the first populist president.

To a room full of bankers, Jackson said, "Gentlemen! I too have been a close observer of the doings of the Bank of the United States. I have had men watching you for a long time, and am convinced that you have used the funds of the bank to speculate in the breadstuffs of the country. When you won, you divided the profits amongst you, and when you lost, you charged it to the bank. You tell me that if I take the deposits from the bank and annul its charter I shall ruin ten thousand families. That may be true, gentlemen, but that is your sin! Should I let you go on, you will ruin fifty thousand families, and that would be my sin! You are a den of vipers and thieves. I have determined to rout you out, and by the Eternal [bringing his fist down on the table], I will rout you out!"[2] What a badass.

The Fed today is far more of a monster than Andrew Jackson

could have ever seen with the Second Bank of the United States. The Federal Reserve, in simple terms, is the system that "creates" money for the federal government. From 2008 to 2014, the Federal Reserve printed nearly $3.5 trillion, yet it is not a bank, and there are no reserves.[3] The money created from the Fed is meaningless, with no standard behind it, and is the direct cause of inflation in this country. If the government needs money, all it has to do is go to the Federal Reserve and ask for it, and the Federal Reserve creates it, without consulting the taxpayer. So artificial dollars are created by the Fed for government use, such as a foreign country offering a bond that the Fed can then turn into American dollars, inflating the money supply, making the dollars you have in your pocket become worth less and less. This is what Milton Friedman meant when he called inflation "taxation without representation." The price of goods and services rises with an inflationary "money"-printing service, yet wages stay the same. You become poorer and poorer, while the elite bankers and businesses benefit, because who benefits from an inflation of price? The same kinds of people who put forward the idea for the Federal Reserve all that time ago in 1913. The government can spend and spend and send themselves deeper into debt because no matter what, the Fed will always find a way to get them more money to waste on nonsense and pseudo-socialist programs, while the burden of this spending falls on you, the taxpayer. Compound this with the fact that because the government has a limitless supply of "money," big banks and businesses can be as risky as they like with their investments because they know the government can always create money to bail them out, and the taxpayer will bear the brunt. "Too big to fail," you say? The only reason why that is true is because you have forced the American taxpayer to make that so. The Federal Reserve was created as a means so Congress could raise an endless amount of taxes through inflation, while the people of America don't even know that they are paying the tax, and the banks can earn unlimited interest on nothing. We are just the suckers for their power-playing money games.

Quantitative easing is how big banks and the federal government work to "fight" recessions. Let's say we are in a recession, and people are not investing or purchasing as much because the market has taken a downturn. This is bad for the overall economy of a nation. So what happens is the Fed comes in and says, for example, *Hey, big bank, how about we give you $600 million of artificial money we print, and then you use that money to invest in the market to help kick-start the economy again?* Well, of course that sounds great to the bank. They just got a copious amount of money for nothing, and are now investing it into a dry market in land, housing, oil and gas, or any other struggling industry around the world. But the problem is, once again, this money is not real. So you have big banks investing fake money into real things, artificially inflating their value. It is a never-ending cycle and does not fix recessions, it crashes economies and keeps the big banks extremely wealthy. In the 1970s we had very low interest rates and the price of everything was rising fast. But what happened when they were forced to raise the interest rates due to inflation? The economy crashed. Does this at all sound similar to the time you live in today? The only difference is that today the debt has absolutely exploded into astronomical proportions where when these interest rates rise again, we could see a market crash that would make the Great Depression look like child's play.

We are in one of the greatest eras of debt in world history because of governments printing this fiat money from central banks around the world.[4] This is not real money. Let me repeat, this is not real money! Central banks create what is essentially fake value to spend on whatever it is they like, sending countries' economies all over the globe deeper and deeper into debt. But someday soon, those debts will have to be repaid, and when that happens, the common man will inevitably be left footing the bill while the big banks and government get off free unless we make sweeping changes to modern monetary policy and end the Federal Reserve once and for all. But I wouldn't hold your breath.

To make matters worse, in 2020, the Federal Reserve hired BlackRock to run the purchases of commercial bonds and corporate mortgages.[5] So what is BlackRock? Blackrock Inc. is the world's largest money manager, and has surpassed over $10 trillion in assets.[6] This is an insane amount of wealth. To put that in comparison, only two countries in the world, the United States and China, have a GDP that is larger than $10 trillion. In other words, BlackRock owns in assets a sum of wealth that is larger than the GDPs of multiple countries combined. You can now see what type of company we are working with here. BlackRock's chairman and CEO is Larry Fink, who was instrumental in the bailing out of major financial institutions during the 2008 financial crisis. A political science major at UCLA who founded Blackrock in 1988, Fink is now one of the most powerful and wealthy men in the world. He has been quoted saying in a speech in 2019, "In this world of anti-globalism...I'm still a globalist and I'm proud of it."[7] How progressive...

BlackRock has its hands in just about everything, and I can guarantee you most of the people who work in different industries all around the world don't even know that BlackRock owns them. Of media companies, BlackRock owns major shares of CNN, Fox Corporation, Comcast, the *New York Times*, ABC, MSNBC, and a myriad of others. BlackRock also has major shares in Pfizer, Moderna, AstraZeneca, and Johnson & Johnson.[8] Energy, finance, housing, media, health, technology, and really any other industry you can think of is tied in some way to BlackRock. The list of companies that BlackRock has shares in could go on for the rest of this book, which is how it has accumulated such massive wealth. But why is it a big deal that BlackRock owns major shares of so many companies? Is that necessarily bad? Well, aside from the fact that it and Vanguard have essentially taken control, or at least partial control, of every industry in America, the ideals that BlackRock pushes couldn't be more emblematic of the progressive, globalist, new world order agenda.

Just in Joe Biden's cabinet alone, three former executives at BlackRock hold key positions.[9] In 2022, Larry Fink wrote an open letter saying, "Every company and every industry will be transformed by the transition to a net-zero world. The question is, will you lead, or will you be led?" How do you think these three executives who serve under Fink are influencing the direction of this country in such prominent roles? When the pandemic began in 2020, BlackRock actually helped the Federal Reserve buy corporate bonds, which essentially was the purchase of corporate debt to bail these companies out.[10] That might sound heroic or noble to you, like it is just BlackRock doing its part to save the world by helping struggling businesses. But what this should really show you is that BlackRock has made our government its bitch. The government needs BlackRock to bail these companies out, otherwise the bureaucracy and scale of government we have achieved could never function. In doing so, BlackRock, with its ownership of countless companies around the world, now owns your government. Chilling, to say the least.

Larry Fink is also a huge proponent of ESG standards within companies. ESG stands for Environmental, Social, and Governance, and is a set of non-financial standards applied to businesses to determine whether or not they are a good investment. This essentially means the more leftist a company is, the higher their ESG score will be. ESG is a type of business social credit system that undermines the real values of a business, whether or not it is a good one. Only a bought-out economist would ever claim that ESG scores are good for the economy, yet Larry Fink in his infinite wisdom knows that these types of scores are beneficial to him and BlackRock. If they are the ones in charge of the scores, then they are the ones who control the market. So a company that owns a share in almost everything, owns our government, and insists on stupefying leftist standards for judging companies is now essentially in control of everything in America. It is laughable when people tell me monopolies are a thing of the past or that "this is the free market at work."

BlackRock isn't the only force at play here. It is deeply connected with the World Economic Forum as well, a group claiming by admission in their mission statement, "The Forum engages the foremost political, business, cultural and other leaders of society to shape global, regional and industry agendas."[11] This is not just some think tank. The WEF by its own statements wants to "shape agendas." The organization is run by Klaus Schwab, who founded it in 1971. He has been the one to popularize terms you may have heard of, such as the "Fourth Industrial Revolution," "stakeholder capitalism," and the "Great Reset." The WEF's board of directors consists of some of the most powerful people in the world, with politicians, bankers, and businessmen taking part. And guess which one of our favorite guys is on their board? Larry Fink! Other members include Al Gore; Mark Schneider, the CEO of Nestlé (one of the most evil corporations on the planet—just look at what it has done with baby formula around the world);[12] Kristalina Georgieva, managing director of the International Monetary Fund; Thomas Buberl, CEO of AXA, one of the biggest insurance companies in the world; Marc Benioff, chair and co-CEO of Salesforce; as well as a myriad of other notable business leaders and people in governments around the world.[13] The list of attendees at WEF forums is even more stacked with powerful people, with presidents of countries, the president of the European Commission and European Parliament, and all sorts of congressmen on both sides of the aisle, among other politicians and business leaders from all over the world.[14] What could all these powerful people possibly be doing meeting with one another?

The Great Reset, despite being called a conspiracy theory by many, was first popularized when Klaus Schwab used it as the title of his 2020 book. Not much of a "conspiracy" when the people at the top name their own books after it...The Great Reset is a plan of action to "revamp and reset" every aspect of our society and economy. The WEF tells us that this reset must take place because our markets are facing inevitable collapse, and the only way out of it is with the restructuring of the world economy. In a post on the WEF site, Klaus Schwab writes, "Every country, from the United States to China, must participate, and every industry, from oil and gas to tech, must be transformed. In short, we need a 'Great Reset' of capitalism." He goes on to say, "The third and final priority of a Great Reset agenda is to harness the innovations of the Fourth Industrial Revolution to support the public good, especially by addressing health and social challenges. During the COVID-19 crisis, companies, universities, and others have joined forces to develop diagnostics, therapeutics, and possible vaccines; establish testing centers; create mechanisms for tracing infections; and deliver telemedicine. Imagine what could be possible if similar concerted efforts were made in every sector."[15] Yes, imagine what could be done if all of the biggest corporations in the world worked with their respective governments and monopolized the market and built even more technological and medical tools to control the population. Wouldn't that be wonderful? If the rollout of Covid vaccines taught us anything, it is that large global efforts of propaganda are extremely profitable and successful when done right. All this Great Reset talk might sound utopian and beautiful, but when these corporations and governments all collude to take your rights away if you do not comply with their new agenda, what happens to your utopia then? What if you don't want to get vaccinated, or have a digital ID, or hand over your property to the government?

Will you even be allowed to disagree with our new "experts" and one-world government? They tell you that "you will own nothing and be happy." Is that the type of life you want to live? Does that sound like a utopia to you?

There is so much to unravel and unpack with the WEF with their influence and connection to BlackRock, the Federal Reserve, and industries around the world and what they plan to achieve, but the key takeaway I hope you all got from this is that you must be self-sufficient. Fighting against the WEF and BlackRock means doing everything you can to be sustainable all on your own. Shop at local businesses, grow your own food, don't take out massive loans from credit card companies, invest your money in small local banks, buy a house and stop renting, get away from the toxicity of major urban areas, focus on your health and nutrition, start a family, buy gold and silver, and stop worrying about your worldly wealth. Focus on the parts of your life that truly matter and don't become a slave to the "hustle culture" mindset we have been led into. The elites want you to believe it is empowering to be the best at spreadsheets and emails in the modern corporate world. There is nothing admirable about being a corporatized cog in a machine. Obviously, everyone has to work to provide for themselves and their family, but making your self-worth and purpose hinge solely on your career and the wealth you receive from it is a one-way ticket to extinguishing your soul.

The state of the world economy and how the elites control us through modern monetary policy keeps me up at night. I fear for the future of this country, and I fear for my future children's and grandchildren's lives in America. To fix these problems, we must return to the gold standard, end the Federal Reserve, get more strict on monopolies, stop revering CEOs and business leaders as our saviors, cap government spending, and become as self-sufficient as we can. We can't escape all the tyranny around us right now, but we all can do our best to become individuals against an economic dictatorship.

Chapter 7

TRANSHUMANISM AND THE FUTURIST MOVEMENT

In Futurism man has completely ceased to be
the leading theme of art, indeed in futurist art there
are literally no more human beings, for man has
been torn into tatters. All the real things in the
world leave the places that are proper to them,
and objects such as lamps, sofas, streets begin to
penetrate the human form, so that man and his
incomparable personality are no longer entities
at all. Man collapses into the world of objects.

—Nikolai Berdyaev

If man can become a god, what does he need God for? Our technological advancements have taken us to heights humans could not even have dreamed of, and in this pursuit of innovation, we have created a world where almost any man or woman can be comfortable, connect to people around the world, and travel anywhere they would like to go. But with these mechanisms, we have indeed constructed hubris within ourselves, and have become insatiable in the face of the ever-expanding prowess of our own machines and technology. We create and create without giving much thought to the repercussions of such creations, and thus, because of our novel inventions and designs, we have placed ourselves at the apex of human history and declared ourselves gods in our own right. We believe because we can create such powers that we ourselves must be all-powerful, but it is only a ruse we tell ourselves to fill the void of the godless society we have created. Technology is no replacement for God, yet we continue to innovate in the hopes of achieving god-like status and control over people. This will be our ultimate downfall, and our pride and technology will destroy humanity as we know it.

I must first state here that not all technological advancements are some great evil. That should be obvious, but I can already see the comments claiming I am a luddite, keen on having us only ride around on horses and churn our own butter. What this requires is a deeper look at the innovations taking place, and how these are indicative of a sick society and where we have gone wrong and are continuing to do so. Medical advancements and surgeries have saved many lives and have made having children easier than ever. People in the West are no longer as prone to severe weather conditions as they may once have been. Communicating with loved ones and family is merely a text away. The world is not starving and hunger across the planet is being eradicated. There are many goods that come from technology, so let us get that out of the way first before diving into what has changed. Many of these advancements, ironically, are the reason why things are progressing in the way they are. We have become so comfortable, and things have become so plentiful and bountiful, that we no longer need to struggle with the tribulations our ancestors did, and so we create technologies that go beyond the scope of what would make a human's life better, into what would make their life simply "easier," or even worse, lazier.

For all of Elon Musk's bravery and his exposing of the corruption of Twitter, I have been skeptical of him for a long time because of his Neuralink technology. I understand there is a celebration to be had over what he has done and appreciation and thanks for what he has shown lurking beneath the Twitter surface, but when does the party end? Are we all now supposed to just forget everything else Elon Musk is doing and pretend he is a new god because he trolls Elizabeth Warren on Twitter? Just like with Trump, and just like with me or anyone else, we must look at the whole picture of the person to really get a grasp on what is happening. No one is infallible, and the richest man on the planet is no exception.

First, Elon Musk has deep ties to the Chinese Communist Party. He has attended and spoken at Chinese artificial intelligence conferences, showing his love for China and new artificial intelligence technology.[1] These aren't just some run-of-the-mill conferences either. They are events tailored to promoting the CCP's agenda, organized by the Chinese government, and the CCP is no stranger to using AI to suppress and destroy its citizens' freedoms. The CCP has used AI technology for its surveillance state against its own people and wants to use it to achieve world dominance. It should be concerning that Elon Musk has been a speaker at these conferences since 2018.

Let us now look at Musk's company Neuralink. One day with this technology, you may not even need to read my books, you can just have AI shoot this book straight into your brain through a little implanted chip. Neuralink is essentially a whole brain interface that will be a network of tiny electrodes that will link up to your brain to then be able to communicate with the world. In the future, you and I could communicate through our brain chips without ever speaking a word out loud with this new brain mechanism. This technology would allow you to communicate with the cloud, computers, and the internet, as well as other people who share the same interface. Does this sound like science fiction to you? Unfortunately science fiction is becoming closer and closer to reality, and human trials are expected to be started in 2023. The company claims that this technology can be used to make people with disabilities able to function normally again, but the implications of these devices go far beyond that, even if we give them the benefit of the doubt and assume their creation is for noble intentions.[2]

Imagine for a moment that you had one of these brain chips installed, and everything you thought and communicated was able to be monitored and logged by the company that owns it. It is one thing to have your social media browsing history monitored, but what about your emotions, private conversations, and thoughts? Then what if that information is sold to China and mega-corporations that bookmark everything you think and use it against you? Imagine if this technology got hacked, and someone stole all of your private thoughts and communications. Imagine if someone wanted to put messaging and an agenda into your interface and brainwash you inside your very mind. They could tell you what to think, what to do, and how to act. You would lose your humanity, you would cease being human, your soul would perish, and you would be merely a slave to the people who own your mind. Add on some new bionic body parts and organs and you have an AI robot that only resembles a human. This is the potential future we are heading for with this type of technology. It is unsafe, there are no laws surrounding it, and it is exploitable by people who want power and control over you.

Much of this new technology we see as exciting new gadgets that are often labeled as human "enhancements," devices that will elevate our bodies and minds to be better than what we started with. I know many get excited and have goosebumps at the thought of these new developments and love the idea that they may be able to replace their arm with a laser cannon or read people's minds, but this is just wishful thinking. The purpose of this technology is not human enhancement, but the destruction of humanity itself. You cannot be a human if your thoughts and emotions are under contract to someone else. If they can turn a technology on, they can always turn it off, and addicting people to their new brain chips and bionic limbs will create a whole generation of people with no notion of the reality of life. They will lose their souls. Being a human means dealing with the limits and complications of the human body that God gave us, not trying to "improve" it through worldly means. We are not immortal, and we are not all-knowing. It is time for humans to realize that again, and reject Neuralink and similar technologies that look to rob us of our humanity.

All of this new technology spawns from postmodernism. Postmodernism is a deconstruction of modernism and premodernism that essentially says nothing is objective, everything can be changed, and ideals, traditions, and notions of the past are merely archaic and must be dismantled. Medieval, biblical, and traditional premodernist values of the past rely on a knowledge of human experience and how people dealt with hardships and turmoil throughout history using intrinsic values from scripture as well as observation of human reality. Chivalry, the roles of men and women, and realistic interpretations of human nature come from premodernism. Modernism was the rejection of many of these values but with a slight reverence to them to not totally destroy the past, while postmodernism is the complete annihilation of history. Whereas premodernism since antiquity believes humans have an intrinsic value, a soul, and are more than just flesh and bones, postmodernism construes humans as purely material objects, able to be molded and bent and changed. There are no static values of what it means to be a human in the postmodernist lens, and everything about a person can be restructured and crafted to fit the current zeitgeist of what people, not God or tradition, view as good or bad.

This is why our current technological advancements are so terrifying, because they are entrenched in the postmodern lexicon. Humans are more than just their skin and organs; they have a soul and a humanity that cannot be seen by the naked eye, but are there nonetheless. Postmodernism is the destruction of this notion, and in conjunction with brain chips, AI, and bionics says we are solely a blank slate to be built upon and enhanced. The Nazi experiments during World War II are the ends of what postmodern thought will bring you: a society that experiments on people for the "growth" of humanity through terror and violence, all in their eyes through the promise of progress. Postmodernism is more than just the destruction of traditional gender roles or the heterosexual nature of man, but a complete breakdown of what it means to be a human, presenting us all as just sacks of meat to be changed for whatever ends the new "gods" of this world find fitting.

Tinder, although unrelated to Neuralink yet totally a postmodern invention, is another new sensation that troubles me. And no, not just because I don't get any matches on there, but because of what the dating app represents. Tinder was revolutionary in the dating app scene as the first mainstream app of its kind to introduce the swiping feature, a means by which users could determine whether they were interested in someone or not in a matter of seconds. Right swipe meant they liked you, left swipe meant they did not. But what is going on behind the scenes that made the app so successful? Why has Tinder made so much money on not just ads, but on their extra perk systems you can buy within the app? It is because at the end of the day, Tinder understands the insecurities of humans, specifically men, and exploits them through the application.

A June 2016 study from Queen Mary University of London pertaining to the Tinder habits of men and women found that women had a 10 percent match rate, whereas men had a closer to 0.6 percent match rate.[3] This means that men are getting likes and matches far less than women, and thus are spending more time on the app swiping and looking for potential dates. Tinder has a feature that lets you purchase the ability be seen first by a hundred people when they first launch the app, yet with men's measly 0.6 percent match rate, that would statistically mean that even after purchasing that perk, you would not even be guaranteed to get an extra match. So with men getting so few matches, coupled with the already declining strength and true masculinity of men in the West today, Tinder makes money off their insecurities and uses their app technology to get men hooked on their product. The promise of a match and the validation of self-worth it gives to a man is a dopamine hit, and is why these swipe-based dating apps can be so harmful to people who spend an excessive amount of time on them. Like a drug, this technology has gotten them addicted to this validation, and thus works to destroy their ability to communicate in real relationships because instead of love, they are only looking to fill that validation void they need filled while swiping on Tinder.

But Tinder makes your life easier, right? No longer do I have to go to a bar, or church, or the park and spark up a conversation with someone of the opposite sex. I can just use a dating app and find someone to go out with so much easier through mutual attraction through text technology. The same can be said about porn as well. Why would I go and spend the time, money, energy, and potential embarrassment of trying to woo a woman to intimacy and romance with me if I can just watch porn on my phone and satisfy myself with none of the heartache or disappointment? Who needs friends when I can have social media likes? Who needs to learn how to cook when I can order all my food directly to my house? Who needs a hobby or passion when there are video games and TikTok?

Technological advancements have become a replacement for human interaction. We are social creatures by nature, and our new innovations latch on to that instinctual need we have to connect with others of our species and use it as a cheap substitute for real attachment. Instead of bringing us together, these new advancements tear us apart, and make us more isolated than ever before. A man before may have courted a woman and swayed her through prose. Now he just sends her a message asking where she is and telling her she's hot. This technology has killed romance and makes every person indistinguishable from the rest, merely a number to be used as a source of false connection and validation for our exploding insecurities.

Much of this newfound technology also exacerbates our laziness and our disconnect from reality. One of the scariest examples of this are the new social robots that you put in your home, such as Embodied Moxie or ElliQ. These robots communicate with you and talk to you and make it seem as if another person is there.

That doesn't sound so bad, right? A robot that keeps your grandma company, or maybe one that serves as a companion for a child who wants someone to play with? On the surface, it doesn't sound so insidious, yet the nefarious nature of machines such as this, whether intentional or not, is far-reaching and disturbing. Just as with the brain chips, these social robots are sending data they collect on you back to a data center somewhere where information about you is harvested and used. These robots are listening to you and watching you with cameras that judge your emotions and language using their natural language processing AI capabilities, and creating a "personality" for themselves to match the person they are with. The robot shows you that it is empathetic so that you divulge your deepest secrets to it, all the while it is recording and storing everything you say and do. Do you see the problem here? They even have the power to surpass humans through higher intelligence and learning capabilities. You really want to put that into your house, watching your every movement and thought? As Steve Bannon says, either we control technology or it controls us.

Let's say for the benefit of the doubt that these robots weren't even collecting any data on you, and were just perfect computer companions that weren't going to hurt you or sell your information. Why would you want it regardless? You cannot replace a friend with a robot, or the touch of a loved one with a machine. These types of machines, whether companions, workers, or anything else that could be seen as a helpful entity for humans, have the power to separate us from all human interaction and destroy what makes humans special. Humans are supposed to work hard, experience pain and loneliness, and deal with problems through their own ingenuity and hardy nature and spirit. Replacing every problem in your life or having every discomfort solved by a machine does nothing to help you grow in your character or as a person. In truth, it makes you lazy, fat, and susceptible to more brainwashing as you no longer have agency to your own thoughts and are merely a slave to the technology you have purchased that you rely on for everything you need.

I always hear people say, "Well, if we had robots to do everything we don't want to do, then we could focus on other things that we are passionate about and not trouble ourselves with doing boring things." This is an asinine argument, and no one really believes it. When you don't have things to do, you procrastinate, and you spend time idly doing things that are nonsense. No one is not "living out their dreams" because they don't have a robot to clean their house, mow their lawn, or be a companion to their grandmother. You aren't living your passions because you are lazy and choose ease of comfort over hard sacrifice time and time again. If you had burning passions and tasks you wanted to accomplish, you wouldn't let the fact that you don't have robots stop you. Great men throughout history didn't let that stop them, and in fact, having robots would only exacerbate the West's ever-present laziness and idleness and just send us back to the couch for more mindless Netflix and junk food. Great, heroic people always find a way to do what they strive for, regardless of the circumstances. Weak people create excuses. Hard work and tenacity are part of the human condition of achieving power over self, and relinquishing these tasks and purposes to robots only further strips us of our humanity and sends us deeper into unbridled lazy chaos.

As you can tell, I am incredibly skeptical of any technology that offers convenience to humans in exchange simply for a monetary value. Again, not all technology of convenience is an evil. A washing machine, a refrigerator, a toaster, or a lightbulb is not some great horror to be feared, but a tool that is helpful for our survival and ability to live fruitfully. But your toaster is not connected to artificial intelligence and it does not take advantage of your insecurities. The toaster does not empathize with you, or promise you a better and easier life, or send back data about you, or sacrifice your ability to connect with others. It toasts bread—that's it. To advance with technology gracefully, justly, and intelligently we must come to grips with our own capabilities and have real, moral discussions on whether or not we should create such technologies, even though we can.

Should we have porn and new sexual technology that alleviates feelings of temporary loneliness for quick pleasure? Or should we try and instead spend our time developing ways that people can build real spiritual and romantic intimacy with each other? Should we have dating apps and social media that make it easy to connect with others out of a craving for affection and camaraderie? Or should we build technologies that encourage real-life conversations based on positive emotions and love? Should we replace our cognition with chips that allow us to communicate via the cloud and electrons? Or should we try and deepen our understanding of other people and converse with those we trust about important and meaningful topics when we can see them face-to-face? Should we abandon work and relegate undesirable tasks to robots and machines, making them our companions in the process? Or do we pick ourselves up by the bootstraps, realizing life is challenging and that we are ready to be strong and steadfast, overcoming our worldly limitations by the will of our spirits?

These are the questions we as humanity must answer. I for one would rather cease to exist before I let my life be dominated by external technologies imagined in some factory in China. You can either embrace difficult tradition or embrace easy modernity. But I can tell you, the hard way is almost always the good way, and is part of the test that will challenge you toward your ultimate self. It is not some fortuitous circumstance that we were put on this earth to deal with hardship and pain; it is in our very nature to do so, as we have been designed to be this way. Anyone who promises some shiny technology as a golden chalice with a promise of grandeur and ease is merely a snake-oil salesman, trying to guarantee you a happiness, serenity, and meaning you never needed from them or their gadgets in the first place. Do not let the technology and transhumanist agenda take hold over you, no matter how exciting and grandiose it may sound. Doing so means sacrificing your very soul for this false holy grail of salvation.

Chapter 8

THE DESTRUCTION OF ART

The development of modern art with its seemingly nihilistic trend towards disintegration must be understood as the symptom and symbol of a mood of universal destruction and renewal that has set its mark on our age. This mood makes itself felt everywhere, politically, socially, and philosophically.

—Carl Jung

Art is far more important than people realize. The art produced today is no longer a reflection of truth to be displayed, but merely a faux derision of art, a cheap replica put in its place, more focused on making a mockery of tradition than creating something enduring and magnificent. Art is not just paintings, but sculpture, words, film, architecture, music, and myths, and all have fallen prey to the modern and postmodern sympathies of our age. For every great and beautiful artistic work that is produced today, there are ten pieces in its place whose value is as fleeting as a comet. There was a time when creation was seen as admirable. Now when I hear someone say they're an "artist" I squirm.

Art is more than just some entity created to be looked at, it is a telling of history and a direct reflection of the culture of the day it was created in. Art holds cultural significance. Taking all of the art movements of human existence and ordering them chronologically is more than an archive of paintings and monuments through time; it is a story of triumphs and losses, of rising and falling cultures, and it showcases the priorities of said society. Art imitates life as it would be, and looking at what influenced the pieces and works of each time showcases what each person or culture cherished or revolted against. Romanticism was a direct statement to the Enlightenment, and was characterized by its focus on individualism, love of nature, and human emotion. That was in direct contrast to the Industrial Revolution transpiring around the

Romantic artists, and their work reflected their feelings about the times. Impressionism was born out of artists wanting to break the conventional rules of art, while neoclassicism embraced Hellenistic styles and ideas as a return to symmetry in art. Whatever the movement may be, the art of the time directly corresponds to the feelings at the time of those who create it, if it is indeed art worthy of being called art. I do not believe in the modern idea of art for art's sake, claiming anything can be art just because someone made it. Which leads to the question: What went so wrong with creativity in the world today?

Modern art was a movement from roughly the late 1800s to the 1970s, and was categorized as a new, experimental type of art. It is a style I find unappealing and trite, where artists stood on the shoulders of the great artists before them and claimed they had done something brilliant. I know it is not some incredibly hot take to throw hatred at modern art, but there is a deeper meaning behind it than just "hey, that's ugly." Modern art distorts reality, and is a clear reflection of modernism itself, which breaks down traditional standards and reconstructs them. Art of the modern age takes man and garbles him, twisting him into "whatever the artist wants him to be." Many pieces of modern art have people displayed grotesquely, with misshapen bodies and faces that don't fall into the "outdated" standards humans have historically been presented as in art. Modern art is focused more on abstraction than reality, and thus can claim that there are no standards of art because all art is an abstraction anyway. All art and beauty is subjective to the modern artist, making the act of critiquing modern art useless in their eyes as it is all merely up to each individual's "interpretation." Nonsense. Anyone can look at a Francisco Goya painting and see something different in it that speaks to them, and maybe some people won't like it, which is perfectly acceptable. But to say that it is *unable* to be really judged because it *only* is up to subjective interpretation is Marxist rubbish. Art and beauty have objective standards, and those who deny this do so at the peril of constructing a world where everything is subjective and nothing can be judged for what it really is, making us unable to appreciate real art and beauty when it is finally presented to us.

Art is supposed to push boundaries, but this is only possible when it is honest. Shall I talk about Tolkien again? Or rather a Tolkien-inspired work, as I use the term "inspired" very loosely. *The Rings of Power*, the most expensive show ever made, was released in 2022 to nearly universal scorn. Yes, of course, the usual paid-off critics liked it, but the fans hated it. The show was supposed to be an adaptation of the appendices of the *Lord of the Rings* novels, depicting stories from the second age of Middle Earth, but it was more like what a progressive who has never left San Francisco thinks a medieval fantasy world would be like.

Tolkien based his original novels on European history, and it is a Eurocentric mythos. You have Rohan somewhat representing the Goths, the Shire representing rural medieval England, and Gondor representing the Byzantine Empire in ways. These ancient cultures were predominantly white, but the social justice warrior filmmakers went woke and took artistic liberties in the name of inclusivity, introducing black hobbits, dwarves, and elves contrary to their depictions in previous films. Some fans accused the film-makers of betraying Tolkien's vision and historical authenticity. Liberal writers online, of course, smeared those voices as racists.

But there are standards of art. And as you can see, these standards are totally arbitrary and applied at the whim of whatever social ideology is hot with the elite at that moment. The creators of *The Rings of Power* obviously care nothing about keeping with the standards of Tolkien's legendarium, but they do care about keeping standards with the leftist social paradigm. This is how art lost its soul. It sacrifices beauty and truth and reflection of humanity for cheap social morality points and spectacle. Just watch any of these latest Marvel adaptations and try and tell me the people who made them loved what they were making or had a reverence for great art and it wasn't just Disney trying to make copious amounts of money. These projects are soulless and vapid at best, and at their worst direct admonishments of the past that only satiate the greed of whoever produced them.

Art is supposed to be beautiful. It is supposed to be something you admire as it tells you something true about your soul and the world. Humans of the past knew this and knew the power of surrounding yourself with beauty. I live in Tampa, Florida, and I sure do enjoy being here. But for the love of God can someone please do something about the architecture here? Except it isn't just a Tampa problem—that goes for most of America and any city around the world with modern construction. After spending large amounts of time in the Netherlands and throughout Europe, you start to understand the power of beautiful architecture around you. A good litmus test for your dates is to ask the person you're with if they would rather see Rome or Dubai. If your date chooses Dubai, I'm sorry but they are not the one. Dubai is a hellhole of modern architecture that displays and presents itself as classy, nuanced, and futuristic. But it is nothing more than slabs of concrete, steel, and glass made into disgusting amalgamations of vanity for the people who designed them. There is nothing beautiful about them and they reflect perfectly what our culture deems as "high-class society." Traditional and classic architecture was made with a knowledge that the things you surround yourself with mean something. Walking into any of the world's oldest Catholic churches is breathtaking, and you cannot help having reverence to God when you walk in. Compare that to one of these megachurches we see today that are nothing more than a box and a door and you can feel the difference. Yes, designing these churches and classical structures is more time-consuming and potentially more expensive, but is it not worth it to have beautiful things surrounding us? Especially when our souls crave more than anything to see some beauty in this world that we sorely lack.

There is a reason, beyond the fact that the building materials are cheap, for the way our structures are designed today. The elites want you to be demoralized. When you walk around a city that is designed with intricacy and care, you feel like an individual. You become happy. But when you see the ugly and cookie-cutter buildings of the present, all you feel is dread. There is no inspiration there. The oligarchy wants you to feel trapped and isolated in the cocoon of concrete around you, and they want you to feel like you can't escape. They don't want you to see wondrous things and be inspired by their luster and majesty; they want you to see ugliness and subjectivity and be a part of the hive like everyone else. A lack of beauty is how the world controllers quell your passion and terminate any stirring of creativity that may be inside you.

The destruction of beauty and art is directly related to post-modernism and Marxism. I mean, there is literally a category of art called postmodern art. In the postmodern worldview, great pieces of art, literature, and architecture from the past are meant to be "deconstructed," and although deconstruction is a pinnacle of critical theory, in which all ideas are meant to be torn apart and slandered, with the Marxists it usually takes on a more literal sense, and great pieces of human history have been lost in the name of "progress." During Mao's Cultural Revolution in China, much was lost. Old buildings were burned to the ground, and great art and tradition of the past were destroyed, all to usher in the new. This is where progress takes you—the annihilation of the old and true.

In America today we have the removal of statues as our cultural revolution, a disgusting practice used by those with feeble minds who can't stand to see history that doesn't align with their university-taught worldview without bursting into anger. If you believe that some of those Confederate soldiers whose statues are being torn down all across this country are the world's most evil villains and you want to see their statues removed because of the historical significance of leaving them up, I can somewhat see a case to be made there, although I vehemently disagree. But the truth is, the people tearing down statues aren't actually offended by the acts of these immortalized men, they are offended that it is a part of our history, and our world today according to them has no need for history if it is white and male. Don't believe me? In 2021, a statue of Thomas Jefferson, one of our founding fathers, a brilliant and honorable man, was removed from New York's City Hall after 187 years because Jefferson owned slaves.[1] In 2020, a statue of Abraham Lincoln with a freed slave was removed in Boston because it made people "uncomfortable."[2]

This is my message to all Americans: If you give those people who want to erase our country an inch, they will take a mile every time. You can't let them have anything. I remember many conservatives when the first Confederate statues were being removed saying, *This is okay, that's all right, they were racists anyway.* And now look at what that type of thinking has wrought; the removal of a statue of the man who freed the slaves! You still think this is just about removing "racist" statues? Of course not. It is about the destruction of tradition, history, and everything that makes America, well, America. They want you to forget the past and all of the glory we had. There is no sincerity in those people who say they want to remove statues because they were racist. It is all a power grab to rob you of your heritage and turn you into a modern American with no sensibilities of history or tradition. Just like in George Orwell's novel *Nineteen Eighty-Four*, where history was rewritten and the old books were destroyed, how can you be inspired to live in anything but a dictatorship if you have nothing to reference and look back on in the past? This is why they destroy everything. So you cannot embrace, respect, admire, or strive toward where you and your country came from. It is evil. And it is Marxist. And it is postmodernism at its purest and most sinister.

One thing many of you might not know about me is that before getting into politics, I wanted to be a music writer/journalist. I really was the perfect lefty college kid. In my freshman year of college I wrote for my school paper as the authority on music, focused mostly on artists from 1945 to 1995. I did throwback album reviews, top ten lists, and features on classic artists and bands or songs. It was a great gig while it lasted, until I got out of my music comfort zone and wrote a piece on the trouble with trans bathrooms; then my school newspaper days were over. But alas, I tell you this to show you that music has always been one of my foremost passions in life. Through the creation of this book, my record player has been spinning all of my favorite bands: the Replacements, the Cure, the Carpenters, Jim Croce, Big Star, America, the Smiths, Fleetwood Mac. All of these bands have kept me company throughout my writing of these tens of thousands of words. I have always turned to music as my escape from the rest of the world. Some people have drawing, nature, or TV. For me it has always been music, and that has been the medium to inspire me more than all others.

I find it paramount that everyone have a medium of art that inspires them. If you're reading this and thinking to yourself that you don't have one, I would suggest spending time trying to find it. Being overwhelmed and taken away by a piece of art is what revitalizes your soul. Whether it is great Christian architecture of the dark ages, statues from antiquity, J. M. W. Turner's paintings,

Oscar Wilde's wordplay, or Johnny Cash's guitar, art gives us life. It speaks to our human nature, our past, and where we still have to go. Reject "art" and works that pervert humanity, and embrace the genius, bravery, and tradition of what came before. Only with that level of appreciation for what came before can you love the things that come now and build something beautiful for generations to see for years to come.

Chapter 9

THE INDIVIDUAL VERSUS THE COLLECTIVE

The most important kind of freedom is to be what you really are. You trade in your reality for a role. You trade in your sense for an act. You give up your ability to feel, and in exchange, put on a mask. There can't be any large-scale revolution until there's a personal revolution, on an individual level. It's got to happen inside first.

—Jim Morrison

The most common question I am asked, on an almost daily basis, is what is the solution for the problems afflicting our country. The majority of people I talk to don't believe voting really matters, or they have lost faith completely in our leaders, or their church is now pro-abortion, or everyone around them is brainwashed, and they have no idea what they are supposed to do. They see their country disintegrating morally, culturally, and fundamentally right in front of them, yet they feel powerless to halt the upheaval of the America that once was. They want to partake in some great battle for the heart of their nation, yet they feel nihilistic, and they have no clue where to even begin to fix America. They believe that they are just one person, and what can one person really do against the leviathan of evil we find ourselves up against?

Indeed, it would be silly to believe that one person could single-handedly dismantle an entire system dedicated to destruction. I am not here to provide you with a bloated, untrue message of hope, telling you that alone you can overthrow the oligarchy and achieve a perfect world. That would be a lie, and I will not instill false hope in you. In all honesty, our country balances on the edge of a knife, and the smallest reaction may bring us plummeting down, and one individual, in solitude, will not change that fact or reset the scales. That is just the reality of the situation, so to fix this country, we must look to other solutions that aren't hinged on a single mortal being the savior.

The silver lining here is that although we often think in terms of large-scale problems we need to fix, the majority of the time it actually comes down our own issues that need to be challenged first. It is very easy to blame everyone around you, or "the system," or your parents, or ideology, and never actually look inward as an individual and think how can we become the best human imaginable. Many times, a person will give themself an insurmountable mountain to climb, such as stopping world hunger, or defeating climate change, or ending Big Tech censorship, or electing only Republicans to office, and because they understand that they cannot fix these problems on their own, they use it as an excuse to not focus on themselves and their own personal failings because they can always blame the massive struggle for their problems. They choose not to direct their energy toward themselves because that is something they are actually in control of, and that responsibility is hard to bear. Instead, they look outward to calamities that they alone cannot solve, using them as a crutch to never have to look in the mirror.

The problem is, human nature always wins. It is why leftist utopias can never work, because no matter how perfect a system is, the depravity of man and his sin almost always takes over. So when we look at outward problems and try to offer solutions that do not take into account human nature, we will almost always fail. This is why the most important thing we can do to solve all of the issues in America is not to look outward, but to look inward at ourselves, as hard as that may be. A nation of good people who think as individuals is the remedy for a broken and lost country. If people choose to actually put the hard work in to demand action, character, and morals from themselves and not just from others around them, then the strong and good can win. Imagine an army of God-fearing, history- and country-loving families who put all their resources and fortitude into creating wonderful communities and selves. That as a solution to the maladies of America sounds far superior to any sort of policy solution some conservative think tank could muster in some gray cubicle in Washington, D.C. Create good people, make them think about individual and small communal values, and your country will fix itself.

Of course, this is much easier said than done. As stated before, human nature almost always takes over, and man continuously reverts to instincts and tribalism. But the problem with our twenty-first-century modern, technological world is that morality, individualism, and goodness are not given as elucidations to the fundamental difficulties facing the West. Instead, we hear that the Republican Party will save us, or a megachurch pastor, or some new ivory-tower-concocted policy decision. There is no doubt that there can be helpful, nuanced ideas that can make the world around us better, but without a nation of good people it is all in vain, because who will uphold the tenets of fairness, liberty, and a republic if the people are not overcoming their human nature and practicing the brave values that the prior generation lived by?

People are molded by their environment and become what they are surrounded with. It is quite easy to think that if you lived in an ancient society you would have stood up against child sacrifice, or that if you lived in communist Russia you wouldn't have snitched on your neighbors or joined the Red Army or committed any evil acts. But this is most likely our hindsight at work, and we have no idea what we would do in such situations or how we would have acted. There is evil in all of us, along with the good, and that evil can overtake anyone when that is all they know.

In his book *Ordinary Men*, Christopher R. Browning outlines the acts of cruelty of Reserve Police Battalion 101, a German police force in the Second World War that participated in the Holocaust. These men were normal men from Hamburg, a city that was historically not very pro-Nazi. Their first mission was the genocide of Józefów, where fifteen hundred people were killed one by one. Only a handful of the men in the battalion took their commanders' offer not to partake in the killing; the others did as they were told. As the war raged on, these men, according to Browning, fell into three different groups. First, only about a dozen of the men made up the group of "Passive Dissenters," who tried to avoid the killings altogether whenever possible. Second were the group of "Willing Killers," who relished the atrocities they were committing and made up about 10–25 percent of the men. Last were the group of "Reluctant Participants," about 75–90 percent of the men, who were repulsed by many of the killings they took part in, but nonetheless murdered anyway. By the end of the war, the Reserve Police Battalion 101 had killed over thirty-eight thousand people.[1]

The story of these men shows us a lot about human nature. If the world around you is pushing you to do something, even commit heinous, evil crimes, many people go along with it because that is what the pervading culture presents. They want to be a part of a group and so they join something they know is not right or good for the sole reason that they can exist by the societal norms of the collective. Yet just because we can understand why a man from Hamburg would join the police battalion and commit such evil does not mean that we excuse him for his actions. If you live in a fallen world and a fallen society, at the end of the day, *you* still have a choice of how to act. You take responsibility for living as an individual, or joining in the collective hive mind. A handful of those German policemen refused to partake in the killings, yet many found their own actions disgusting and reprehensible but did them anyway for fear of retribution and isolation. What will you choose? Everyone always has a choice to be good and to be an individual. You have to take responsibility.

In our world today, your choices may be less black-and-white than that of massacring civilians or becoming a pacifist, but that does not mean there are not hard choices to make to reach individuation. Every day you have a myriad of decisions to make to go along with the herd and groupthink, each alternative a sacrifice of your collective spirit and lack of acceptance from the masses. Do you partake in the mundane conversations of your tribal group, or do you stretch your mind beyond the perimeter of others' mental boundaries? Do you seek to behave as your neighbor, a colleague, or a celebrity, or do you usher in a new form of living not dependent on the satisfaction of others' opinions? Do you join in the evil surrounding you because it is "normal," or do you strive to be better than what the culture has said is okay?

Both the Democrats and the Republicans want you to think in terms of collective values. It is how they achieve their power and wealth, and without a mass of followers they cannot retain their grip on control. The real individual stands alone and does so proudly due to the pursuit of truth. Marxism, the quintessential utopian ideology, wants you to think within the collective as well, as a plebeian who stands up against the upper classes and strips power from their grasp. Have you ever noticed how all of these political, economic, and social ideologies always put you into some sort of group concoction? Instead of telling us a way to live as individuals, these systems hinge on uniting massive groups of people under their common purpose. Of course, large groups of people with a common *good* purpose can be incredibly powerful and useful for acts of valor, but the ideologies themselves that supplant your individuality with that of merely a soldier for the person who instituted the groupthink in the first place is no collective you want to be a part of.

Collectivism is powerful. It is how the Nazis, the Soviets, the Mongols, and every other destructive force throughout history took power. Massive amounts of groupthink and collectivism are usually a sign of a sick society. Large amounts of populism, ideas concerning "the people" and anti-establishment and anti-elite themes, are usually signs of decay in a society. A healthy community with just and chivalrous rulers does not resort to populism, only a sick one does. Donald Trump won the presidency in 2016 and rallied such ardent support all over the world because of his populist message. What does that tell you about the state of America today that we elect someone like Donald Trump? If we had glorious and fair leaders we would never elect someone with a message like Donald Trump, but we did so because he was needed to combat the elitism and selfishness of the ruling class.

Populism is merely a form of collectivism and should not be

viewed as a superior political ideology, because it always comes up short, as it often misses the ideas of individualism the human spirit needs. Populism is not *inherently* good, because humans are naturally hierarchical, and hierarchies are not evil just because they exist. That would be the Marxist way of thinking, that all struggles are a class struggle and based on power structures. In nature, the strong lead and dominate the weak, and in a good human society, the leaders help the followers achieve greatly, but they aren't supposed to dominate them. Populism arises when the latter inevitably happens and when the lower classes become too comfortable not being individuals. It is why the two most popular political candidates in this country in 2016 were both populists, Bernie Sanders and Donald Trump. Both appealed to the lack of agency and strength the masses had over their own lives. Yet instead of turning toward building themselves away from ideology and tribalism altogether, they came to a head with two opposite political, populist notions. Yet today, even after all the populist movements of the late 2010s, and even earlier with the Tea Party, our world is more nihilistic than ever. Being a part of any group, conforming to it, and attaching it to your identity for an extended period of time is a one-way ticket to soul starvation, and you become merely another foot soldier in the caravan and find yourself no closer to achieving a sense of individual nirvana and self-overcoming. Collectivism, communism, political party idolatry, and populism are all symptoms of a society that sacrifices the inherent value of the individual and the natural order of life in favor of groupthink and selfishness.

Every time you latch on to one of these collective identities without much thought, you also pigeonhole yourself with every other member of that group and its leaders. If you become a Democrat, it is likely that someone like me would probably think you're vaccinated against Covid, support gay marriage, are "anti-racist," love Joe Biden, and are probably someone I don't want to spend much time with just based on group ideology alone. But all of that could be untrue. You could really be an anti-vax hippie who sees people with love and thinks Joe Biden is terrible, yet because of the group identity you have latched on to feel like you are a part of something you are now seen as something entirely different by others. Placing these labels on yourself is a good way to be accepted by people in your group, but it isolates you from all the wonders of all the other people out there. When it comes to the left, straying at all from their dogma is an automatic separation from their group, and not toeing the line even a bit will have you excommunicated and canceled. There is no room for free thought.

Joining the groupthink means you are then also tethered and responsible for the words and actions of its leaders. I can't tell you the number of times people have commented to me online about some political issue and said I must agree with Trump's stance on it simply because of the fact that I have historically been a Republican voice, whether I agree with Trump's policy or not. Yet because I am a part of this group, I am now tied to anything the leader of said group does, even if I don't agree. This isn't always a bad thing, of course, if the leader of the band is marching toward a noble aspiration that you wholeheartedly agree with, but many times in the eyes of the world you now have to be on the hook for their blunders and things you don't agree with simply because you gave up your individual spirit for collective ideology. It is a slippery slope, and is a balance of separation and acceptance you have to actively think about and act on.

Collectivism and social cohesion only truly work when you have a group of people who are first and foremost individuals before they are whatever entity they have attached themselves to. Many of these ideologies will tell people they need to be a part of whatever group in question to fight for "the greater good." I am sure you have heard that one before. When it came to Covid, you had to lock down and get vaccinated for "the greater good." When it came to sending billions of our hard-earned taxpayer dollars to Ukraine it was for "the greater good." When dissidents got censored and banned from social media sites it was for "the greater good." These are all a farce. More damage has been done in the name of "the greater good" than any other ideology in human history. Communist upheaval in Russia was for the greater good, along with the Roman welfare state, the Salem witch trials, Nazism in Germany, FDR's New Deal, LBJ's Great Society, and countless other examples where the leader of said society herded the people together like sheep and made them believe their actions were actually for the benefit of the people. As Albert Camus said, "The welfare of the people in particular has always been the alibi of tyrants, and it provides the further advantage of giving the servants of tyranny a good conscience." By telling people they must join together behind some "noble" cause for the greater good, shaming those who don't join as unpatriotic and weak, you get an army of identical slaves at your disposal ready to have their identities hijacked for whatever purpose you would have them serve.

The elites know that if they can define groups and tell people that by being a part of one they are fighting for the greater good, then they can control them. Think of the LGBTQ community, the triple-vaccinated community, the Black Lives Matter community, or the Zelensky supporter community. The people who are part of all these groups, many times with much crossover, think that they are fighting a system of oppression because they have been given their collective purpose by the culture. Yet instead, these people have become merely pawns in a greater design of social control constructed by the elites, and have in turn fashioned themselves as the new conquistadors of free thought and individualism. They use their group identity as their truncheon, bludgeoning those who stand in their way, all the while thinking they are the oppressed, downtrodden group merely trying to survive. But the power goes to their head, and like the German police battalion, many of them become in a sense "willing killers," finding joy in their new position of power with their brothers in arms. With their new identity, safety in numbers, and the cultural lexicon positioning them as the morally superior force, these collective groups are poised to take over all facets of American life, and if you don't join one of the established groups, you are shunned and seen as evil by those living within them.

When everyone around us is performing in one of these collectives, it can be hard for us not to feel left out—not just when it comes to political theory and ideas either, but with everything in our lives. I know what it's like to see people going out to bars or wasting time and then becoming a different type of person when you are conforming to what your group would like. I know that in my life I did a lot of things and spent a lot of time and money on things I didn't really like, but I thought other people would like me more if I did them. It is the old trope about fitting in all over again. Sure, your mom has said it to you a thousand times, but please take it from me: Your life improves when you stop trying to live part of some manufactured identity to be identical to your peers politically, ideologically, socially, fashionably, spiritually, or sexually. There is a lot of pressure to conform to the world and people around us, and knowing what is right or good for you often conflicts with what society asks of you. You must have more willpower and courage than they do. You must build your confidence and integrity so that the opinions of others don't tear you apart. You must be willing to stand alone and lose what worldly satisfactions you have gained.

Just being a conservative is not enough to make you stand apart as an individual. "Conservatives" are a dime a dozen these days, and it seems like every twenty-year-old kid with an Instagram account and a YouTube history of Ben Shapiro videos is now a conservative influencer or memer. You must *live* as a conservative and a free thinker. A staff member at PragerU used to tell the story of his kids when he asked them why they were conservative, and they said "low taxes." The kids were thirteen. What does a thirteen-year-old child know about taxes? This funny story shows how deep groupthink can go, and that even in conservatism people latch on to ideology just because it seems cool or makes them feel a part of something. You must practice what you preach. Of course, you will have setbacks and won't live some perfect conservative life—God knows I haven't—but you must strive for that if you are trying to break free from the grip of the oligarchy. Remember, the elite want you to be a part of a group ideologically, but they don't want you to actually act on it. Being an individual as a conservative is hard, as is being a true follower of God, but it is the only way to unshackle yourself from collective identity and become you.

The greatest men ever to exist were not put in the history books because they did what was normal. They are not remembered for their bravery and strength because they thought and existed like everyone else. They are not heralded as champions of humanity for their likeness to others. They are immortalized because they separated themselves from everyone else's ways, from identity, and from the limitations society put on them. So be like no one else! Sail for far horizons that others won't tread, and don't let yourself become a slave to the groupthink of the elite. You are more than the standards of our culture that tell you that you must conform or be shunned. In truth, what you must come to realize is that if we live in a failing society, then being shunned and separated from its ways is the best action you could truly ever take for yourself, and you should revel in the fact that you are now on your own, not tied down to the expectations everyone else has placed on you. Do not be placated by simple worldly acceptance. Reach individuation.

Chapter 10

THE BEAUTY OF UNPOPULAR OPINIONS

It is better to go wrong in your own way
than right in somebody else's.

—*Fyodor Dostoyevsky*

If men never stood up with unpopular opinions, there would be no West as we know it. There would be no America as we know it. Brave men and women with rare and unpopular notions created what we love and cherish about the West now. And although at the time many of these people with different thoughts were condemned for their ideas, many of them are now heralded as great thinkers and revolutionaries for what they accomplished, believed, and dreamed.

Being alone is many people's greatest fear. Whether that is no friends, no family, no social status, or no loving relationships, the terror of isolation is a fear for almost all of us. Social media only exacerbates this problem by making it feel like we must always be connected in some way to other people, but at the root of it, it is in our human nature as a social species. Humans have evolved in a way to make us cherish our social groups and connections and use these relationships to build stronger units and survive against the tempest that is the outside world. But what happens when much of the group around you not only stops being beneficial, but becomes detrimental to your creative flourishing and your spirit?

Throughout history, great people have had to stand up against the prevailing culture to achieve something brave and special. Abraham Lincoln is one such person, exemplifying what it meant to be hated for the right and good unpopular stances.[1] When the

Civil War started, the Union had more resources, more men, and more money than the Confederacy. When you looked at the metrics, the Union should have been winning the war from the outset, yet despite all this, they were losing. General Robert E. Lee was a brilliant Confederate commander and his forces were winning battle after battle.

Even as the losing war raged on, tragedy struck Lincoln as his son Willie died of typhoid fever in February 1862. Lincoln's wife, Mary, was inconsolable, and the pain took a huge toll on the president as well. Lincoln was losing the war, his son had just died, and he was trying to be president all at the same time. This was an incredibly stressful and difficult time for him.

It wasn't until Lincoln saw his wife being helped by a Union nurse that things changed for him. This nurse's name was Rebecca Pomroy. Lincoln noticed Rebecca acting jovial, cheery even, when he saw her, despite the fact that she was widowed and the country was falling apart around her. One day, Lincoln asked her how she could be so happy with so much pain around, and she told him it was because of God. Rebecca introduced Lincoln to God at a new level, as beautifully noted in a letter she wrote to a friend: "Dear Mrs. F., how mysteriously God works. Two years since, in the seclusion of my little home, I was encouraging my husband to have confidence in God when the time of our separation should come, and now it was given me to tell Mr. Lincoln in my poor, weak way how wonderfully the Lord had sustained me and brought me out of darkness into light. I bade him take courage in this his time of trial, when God was preparing him to stand firm in duty for the salvation of his country. I shall never forget how the tears coursed down his cheeks as I spoke of God's love in affliction, and I besought him to cast his burden upon him. He told me on parting that he enjoyed my visits, to come often, and he would see me home."[2]

After the president met and conversed extensively with Rebecca, he became a new man, a godly man. In his second inaugural address, he said in his speech, "'Woe unto the world because of offenses! For it must needs be that offenses come; but woe to that man by whom the offense cometh!' If we shall suppose that American slavery is one of those offenses which, in the providence of God, must needs come, but which, having continued through His appointed time, He now wills to remove, and that He gives to both North and South, this terrible war, as the woe due to those by whom the offense came, shall we discern therein any departure from those divine attributes which the believers in a living God always ascribe to Him?" In the first years of the war, Lincoln had no intention of ending slavery in America, and the Civil War was not just about slavery. Yet now in his second inaugural address, he argued that both the North and the South were being punished by God for the institution of slavery, and that this great evil must be put to a stop, with both sides coming together to agree to it.[3]

For the time in which this happened, this was a grave statement. Although slavery mostly existed in the lower half of the country, racism at the time wasn't just confined to the South. Many white northerners were racist too, or at the very least supported slavery. A copious number of people condemned Lincoln and told him that making the Civil War about slavery was wrong. His cabinet advised against it. Even his wife told him not to do it.

But Lincoln knew the truth, even though he was standing alone against all odds, and in what can only be described as a miracle, the Emancipation Proclamation was signed, the Union won the Civil War, and Lincoln, the first Republican president, is today remembered as one of the greatest men ever to live and is seen as a true hero by millions across America. Abraham Lincoln with his courage and tenacity is an inspiration to us all.

The founding fathers were a handful of men with a brave and brilliant idea to depart from the British Empire and start their own country. This was unpopular at the time, and many Americans actually fought for the British. Support for the war among the colonists never even reached past 45 percent, not to mention the fact that only 3 to 6 percent of the colonists actually fought in the Revolutionary War.[4] Yet the revolutionaries won the war regardless, and America, the world's greatest country ever to exist, was created because of the unpopular belief that man should be free, and that God wanted Americans to be free. It is because of unpopular opinions that you are able to read the unpopular opinions in this book today.

Cancel culture is a cancer on our society and the alibi of the weak and insecure. Only someone who has mediocre confidence and ability would actively look to cancel or, worse, destroy the lives of people who say something that detracts from their worldview. Saying the "wrong thing" and walking on eggshells is now an everyday continuum of thought not just for public figures, but everyone living in the West today, and the fear of cancellation is a driving factor in how we all act and live. It is only weak people who see someone else's opinion and think this person should no longer be able to speak. These are people so flimsy in their own self-worth and ideas that they must take away others' abilities to converse and partake in discussion because they are not strong enough to be challenged. Aside from ideas like pedophilia or direct threats of violence, almost any idea should be able to be discussed. Even if there are social repercussions for the ideas someone presents and people find those thoughts disgusting or completely backwards, there is a place for most everything to be challenged. An atheist should listen to a Christian to better understand their atheism. A vaccinated individual should be open to hearing the literature from someone who despises the vaccine. Hell, all of us should at least be hearing out the flat-earthers to further solidify our belief in a globe.

This is called maturity and self-assurance. Being an adult means you can hear the opinions of others and not throw a tantrum because you disagree. A mature person realizes that hearing opposing beliefs challenges your assumptions, makes you stronger, and hardens your own convictions. We should all be outwardly actively looking for people who disagree with us to further our pursuit of knowledge and truth and not seeking to destroy the lives and careers of others because they think differently. Even if the left plays by the standards of cancel culture, and we lose ground because their mob rule threatens us, we cannot sacrifice the integrity we have to act as they do. I would rather have a smaller company of people with integrity who don't act like children than a group of "conservatives" who want to go canceling everyone on the left because they do it to us. Rise above and be better and don't fall to their level, even if it means losing on worldly cultural grounds. At the end of the day, your integrity is all you have. Don't squander it.

The people whose voracious appetite for destruction, with lives dedicated entirely to the silencing of others, are those with little to no integrity. Early in January 2023, a woman named Kara Lynne was fired from her job from the video game company Limited Run Games because a trans activist demanded the company fire her or lose his support. Why? Because she followed the popular right-wing accounts of Ian Miles Cheong and Libs of TikTok on Twitter. According to *The Post Millennial*, Limited Run Games announced that Lynne had been fired and wrote, "LRG respects all personal opinions, however we remain committed to supporting an inclusive culture. Upon investigating a situation, an employee was terminated. Our goal as a company is to continue to foster a positive and safe environment for everyone."[5] They are saying out loud what we have expected to be true about these companies all along: that they think conservative ideas are "unsafe" and the only ideas that are allowed to exist are those on the left. What is worse, as *The Post Millennial* reported, is that this trans activist posted online about how teens can consent to sex with adults.[6] Where was their cancellation? Seems like evil is allowed to be the popular opinion and face no repercussions, but people with any ideas even resembling conservatism or goodness in general are seen as enemies and must be punished.

This is just one of many examples of people getting canceled for what would seem like innocuous beliefs yet are deemed abhorrent and unforgivable in the eyes of the mob. People get canceled every day for their beliefs, yet the way people handle it usually says more about their character than the cancellation itself. We all know the dog and pony show by now. Someone says something unbecoming or unflattering or that could be deemed as offensive, the mob comes after them (or in many cases just a small, very vocal legion of harpies), and then once they see the backlash they are getting, then comes the crocodile-tears apology. "Hi world, I am so sorry for my comments on [insert hot topic political or social issue]. I deeply regret that I may have hurt [insert minority group] with my words. I did not realize the effect these words can have. Moving forward, I will work to be more careful and never offend anyone with my words again." Blah, blah, blah. Does anyone ever really believe these half-baked cookie-cutter apologies? These are the types of responses the professional, technological world demands of us for compliance with the social norms, not the heartfelt, I-have-wronged-someone-and-seek-repentance type of apology people would actually find convincing. It is all a trite parcel, delivered whenever necessary for the smallest transgression that the elites demand an expression of regret for.

Telling the people demanding remorse from you to kick rocks is the only acceptable way to deal with cancel culture. Timothy Gordon was a high school teacher at Garces Memorial High School, a private Catholic school in Bakersfield, California. Gordon made comments about Black Lives Matter, calling it a terrorist organization. After his comments made the rounds at his school, a petition was created demanding his termination. Shortly afterward, Gordon was fired from his job. At this point, he could have gotten down on his hands and knees, apologized, and begged forgiveness from the school and his peers, exclaiming how he would never say anything unbecoming of BLM again and that he was a changed man now. But he didn't do that. He did interviews and wrote more books, even nabbing a foreword by Michael Knowles in one of them. He didn't apologize to the mob. Yes, he lost his job, but he kept his integrity and is now successful in other ventures he is a part of. He decided he didn't want to be put in a position where he had to sacrifice what he believed in for the sake of other people when what he was saying was true. Mob justice is not real justice, and he knew that, and the unpopular opinions that he never faltered on brought him to the place he really wanted to be.[7]

Every time I have had hit pieces come out against me, or the left (or right) has tried to cancel me, I turn it into a laughing matter. I make fun of the people trying to do so, because there is no other way. I can either come out and say I am sorry and grovel for whatever I said that offended them, or I can stand behind what I said and not cave to their demands. Which sounds better? They don't *really* want an apology from you when you say something they don't like, they want silence and obedience. *Don't you dare speak on something we don't accept as truth or we will destroy you.* Learn that lesson, apologize, and never do it again is their mantra. If people make real mistakes and explicitly act in vile ways then apologies and changes in behavior are necessary for that person to grow and remedy relationships with people they might have actually hurt. But to just apologize for the hurt feelings of some weak-willed person who can't stand ideas existing other than their own or for the powers that be so they know you are submissive to them is a complete joke. We live in a world where you are supposed to have these unspoken manners about offending others, but these are not manners of chivalry and mutual respect, they are merely theater with people acting out their roles. All of it is fake, all of it is a façade, and the way to rebel against cancel culture is to refuse to acknowledge the insecure vultures who demand your total compliance. Do not comply with the scripted apologies they have created for you, and laugh in their faces when they demand it. They have no power over you unless you give it to them.

An opinion is not always good because it is unpopular, but the fact that so many popular opinions are so uncontroversial is unsettling. We in America have become stagnant with the status quo, content with the conformist opinions of our time. We do this at the risk of nothing, but the risk of everything. In gaining worldly acceptance and thumbs-up from everyone around us for thinking how they want us to, we ultimately end up losing ourselves and become nothing more than the flesh and bones that make us. We are more than what we have become. I believe that we as Americans can take the now unpopular ideas this country was founded on with bravery and resilience and present them to the world with a revival. But it takes our rejecting cancel culture and not playing by the tenets of the elites' authority. Only when we realize that it is not just okay but noble to speak uncomfortable truths will we be able to reclaim what was stolen from us. That is the idea that America was founded on; the idea of freedom of speech and no ideological safe spaces. Come to terms with the fact that many will hate you for what you believe, but if the truth is with you, does that really matter?

Chapter 11

NO COMMON GROUND WITH PEOPLE WHO HATE US

The cost of freedom is always high, but Americans
have always paid it. And one path we shall never choose,
and that is the path of surrender, or submission.

—*John F. Kennedy*

If the devil walked into your house right now, what would you do? Would you greet him and hang his coat up for him? Would you tell him to make himself at home? Would you offer him a drink and a place to sleep? Well, there are three possible scenarios for what could occur here. One, you do not know he is the devil, and you let him in as a friend. Two, you let him in out of fear for what he might do if you are not generous. Or three, you deny him entry and banish him from your home. There is only one right answer here. You must at all costs not break bread with the devil and not let evil enter your household.

So why is it that when we see evil around us, we concede to it and allow it to fester? Why is it that when we talk to people who harbor and promote evil and malicious ideas, the right consistently insists on finding "common ground"? Why do we constantly cater and kowtow to the side that would never do the same for us?

In early 2022, I was able to travel to Europe for the first time and speak all across the continent. I went to the Netherlands, Romania, France, Monaco, Germany, and Hungary, and I got to see the Old Continent for what it really was, not just hear about it or see videos online. Aside from the new modern buildings they had built, transforming many old cities into what looked like any other ugly city around the world, Western Europe was undoubtedly remarkable and breathtaking, with history gracing you everywhere you went. But when I went to Eastern Europe, it was like being in a different world. All around Cluj, Romania, were ugly and sad communist buildings, bygones of the past terror that took place there, yet still standing as a constant reminder to what had once been. I found it difficult not to be depressed seeing them everywhere we went. But what was even more heartbreaking was that downtown in one of the main squares was a Che Guevara coffee shop, a café idolizing the Marxist leader who was responsible for the deaths of thousands, who preached an ideology that had destroyed the Romanians' country just years earlier. Had they already forgotten everything that happened to them? Was the constant visage of the buildings and desolation not enough to make them remember what tragedy had once taken place there? It was shocking, to say the least, but heartbreaking more than anything.

When I went to Budapest, I was able to visit the House of Terror, a museum dedicated to the atrocities of the Nazis and communists who ravaged Eastern Europe. It was the most brutal museum I had ever been to. The images and stories depicted didn't hold anything back, showcasing the carnage and destruction Eastern Europe dealt with due to communism during the last hundred years. When I asked Hungarians and Romanians about their parents' or grandparents' stories of the time, there was a surprising consensus: The Russian communists were worse than the Nazis. They said that when the Germans came through their towns and villages, they knew what to expect. They were orderly and did their killing and roundups according to a system and plan. But when the Russians came through during the tail end of World War II, they destroyed everything. They raped every woman in sight, pillaged and burned every town, and caused massive casualties every time they passed a settlement. There was no orderly conduct. They were war-hungry animals, and the way they dealt with the Eastern Europeans under communist rule was no different. They were brutal and terrible, and ruled with an iron fist, where no disagreement or questioning was tolerated.

Communism is an insidious ideology that over the last century killed over a hundred million people.[1] That is a truly unquantifiable number, especially when you take into consideration not just the deaths, but the wounded, the raped, the sick, and all of the other millions affected: mothers separated from their children, husbands who lost their wives, and friends who would never see each other again. The system caused great poverty and inequality everywhere it was implemented, and was a force of destruction, death, and heartbreak around the world during the Cold War. Communism is not just some political ideology with strengths and merits to be examined by some ivory-tower professor. It is an evil, selfish system that tricks the masses into believing that it can save them from poverty and lack of power, when in reality it can only lead to instability and death. Yet with all this evidence to show how desolate communism can be when truly enacted, we still have communists in America and throughout the West who herald it as the savior of our nation and the only way to lift up the lower classes against an oppressive oligarchy.

I am sure many of you have met some of these communists and have tried to debate with them about the terror that was inflicted during those years and what that ideology has wrought. Some of you may have even read my first book, *How to Win Friends and Influence Enemies*, and taken the notes and questions from the chapter on communism to use in these conversations. But alas, even if you have influenced your enemies, the ideology of communism is still alive and well today and growing in the West despite its atrocities, despite its failures, despite its nature, and despite its history. Why is it that evil ideas are allowed to fester and grow and infect our people, seemingly taking away their rationality and turning them into martyrs?

Well, communism as an ideology is a zero-sum game. You either have communism or you don't, and to achieve it in practice takes a complete overhaul and overthrowing of the current status quo and government system. Not much room for compromise there, as you can imagine. When you think of the gender ideology debate, or the war on children, the left also has no room for compromise. It is either let children "fully express themselves" as the gender they claim to be, or you are a transphobic bigot who denies people's existence as the gender they "were really born." How about Covid and the lockdowns? If you had even a question about the safety or the efficacy of the vaccine or masks you were a science-denying, Grandma-killing conspiracy theorist, and it was either the Covid fanatics' way or risk losing everything.

What I am getting at here is that the left does not compromise on any issue, and what I have come to realize since the publication of my last book is that leftism cares about power over all else, and compromise or facts are irrelevant to the person who holds the whip. You can cry facts and logic all you want at the left's tactics and policies, but when the leftist punches you in the face "illogically," it doesn't really matter that you proved them wrong, does it? Winning the debate with a gunman doesn't affect the fact that you are still staring down the barrel of a rifle from someone who wants to see you dead. Power through force is the left's only goal, and if the right doesn't come to realize that soon, we will continue to be rolled over by the leftist machine.

A leftist doesn't care about you calling them out for their hypocrisy, because hypocrisy is not a force that can be used to stop their power. For example, transgender women can't get pregnant because they don't have a uterus, yet what happens when we call them out on this for their hypocrisy? They double down and say men can menstruate. This is absolute idiotic lunacy, yet despite conservatives pointing out the hypocrisy and the lies, the narrative persists, and is now more prevalent than ever, even transferring over to children and their gender ideologies. Noting their hypocrisy or posting facts and logic on social media doesn't change the fact that pediatricians are handing out puberty blockers like candy and cutting the breasts off young girls to let them be whatever gender their parents or teachers probably pushed them into. In fact, in some cases it emboldens them, because they then know whom to label as bigots and transphobes. If the leftist owns the doctor's office, your remarking on the flaws in their logic won't stop them. The only thing that stops them is getting that doctor's office shut down and revoking the medical license of the sick doctor who performed those surgeries in the first place. Power must be used to stop power. A wild mustang must be broken in, not coaxed with reasoning as to why it should let you ride it. Conservatives must go on the offensive and attack the left's ideas head-on, not just try and disprove them through idle messaging and talk.

"But Will," you ask, "didn't you write a whole book before on how to change people's minds and bring them over to our way of thinking? Are you now saying that is the *wrong* thing to do?" Well, my friend, yes I did, and all the arguments in that book still stand. Those questions to ask and facts to weave in are for individual conversations and grassroots organizing. But when it comes to ideologies as a whole and our war against them, we must be unflinching and understand the dynamic we are working in. We should be having conversations with as many individuals as we can to try and dissuade them from leftism or simple ideas, that is what we are called to do, but the oligarchy will not be dismantled just because we are right and factual. The people at the top do not need to have conversations, because they are already in charge. The men sentenced to the Siberian gulags were *right* that it was immoral for them to be there, but it didn't stop the fact that they were freezing to death, their backs breaking under the heel of the communists. There is no in-between. We either lose to the communists and new high-tech feudal overlords, or we beat them. I, for one, am ready to win.

Many people may be reading this chapter as harsh. "Will, you are just dividing us further! We can't have unity with rhetoric like this!" And if that is what you thought, then you would be correct. Tell me, where was "unity" when people lost their jobs because the government locked us all down? Where was "unity" when families and spouses couldn't visit their loved ones because they were unvaccinated? Where was "unity" when I spoke at a school board here in Tampa about a grotesquely vulgar and disgusting book that taught children how to use gay sex apps with adults? There was no "unity" there. Every time I spoke up about any of these evils or when thousands of others did, the left didn't call for us to come together to find common ground. They beat us into submission and got their way whether we liked it or not. People have still not recovered economically from the lockdowns and business shutdowns of the Covid pandemic. As of this writing in late 2022, people can still not enter the United States unless they are vaccinated against Covid. The school board I spoke at unanimously decided to keep the book at that middle school, and many Tampa residents labeled me as a bigot. I do not *want* unity with these people. I want to see them lose power and have good triumph over evil.

Many of these ideas plaguing our society now *are* evil. There are many debates that are merely differences of opinion, such as speed limits, the amount you pay on property taxes, pineapple on pizza, and so on. The people who think pineapple belongs on pizza are not evil, they just have a different outlook and taste from you. That is normal and healthy and brings society to greater heights when opinions and ideas can be questioned fully and discussed completely openly. But there are evil ideas and systems at work in America today, and they are not a matter of opinion. With everything I talked about regarding communism earlier in this chapter, is there any doubt that the ideology is greedy, selfish, and evil? I think any idea that leads to the death of a hundred million people is probably okay to call evil, and I have no qualms about saying so. Sexualizing children is evil. Forcing on people a vaccine you didn't test fully that you know has adverse side effects is evil. Taking advantage of your own citizens is evil. You do not cater to "differences of opinion" with evil. Evil ideas must be eradicated and shut down before they can infest our country further.

You do not find common ground with communism. What do you want, a half-democratic, half-communist world? That doesn't work. You don't find common ground with the ideas surrounding the sexualization of children and their insane gender ideology. All you will get is arbitrary age limits for when it *is* okay to castrate young boys and girls. You don't find common ground with ideas that want to take your God-given rights away. All you will find is a compromise that makes you less free than before. The answer to evil is all or nothing, and we can't give it an inch, not even one. In our world today, it is all about "my truth" and "your truth" and subjective good. But the truth is not subjective. Good and evil are not subjective. To have a society where we cannot define the pillars of each makes for a society where evil and lies always win, because the evil liars will always claim that lies are *their* truth, and that evil is *their* good. Evil must be vanquished, not tolerated, especially given that the same people telling you their evil ideas are right would never try to find common ground with you. They hate your ideas, they look down on you, and they want to see what you love and believe in completely and utterly destroyed on this earth.

So this all begs the question: How do I know if an idea is evil, or whether it is just a matter of opinion? Well, the quickest way to find out if something is evil or not is probably to see if George Soros has donated to a cause that supports it, but since you can't always find that information, the best, and really only way, is through God's word in scripture. In chapter 14 of this book, "God

Save America," I will discuss how this is done and how our country needs God now more than ever to save it, but the long and short of it is that the Bible will have the answers you are looking for, and will help you distinguish your ideas and judge the world precisely.

The elites of this country hate you for what you believe in. They hate your belief in a higher power. They hate your idea of absolute truth. They hate that you aren't terrified to death of a virus. They hate your love of country and history. They hate your sense of community. They hate your love of good things. We do not find common ground with evil people who want total dominion over our lives and who hate us and our values. If you want a good society, don't let the devil walk in and have a seat at the table. Compromising with evil is why people are so apathetic about politics. They see the Republicans as exactly the same as Democrats, compromising and finding "common ground" instead of fighting for the truth. Sure, being uncompromising will make you a lot of enemies, but those are the enemies you want to have. We should be judging our leaders *by* their enemies, not the people they greased palms with. If you have a leader who is well liked by everyone, rest assured you can probably assume they sold out somewhere to get that status.

You can be merciful while also administering judgment. All ideas and all people must be looked at through this lens. The modern Christian lexicon has told us judgment is bad and mercy is always preferable, but this is a fault. You must be able to discern clearly and judge people and ideas accordingly and categorize them for what they are. The hand of mercy having more value than the hand of judgment is what has gotten us into the place we are politically and socially in the first place. The two should be in equilibrium, and both used when appropriate. If you cannot judge the world around you and the ideas presented to you for what they really are, then you will get steamrolled time and time again by the people who abandon mercy altogether. Evil ideas exist, and although people can have moral ambiguity and grayness themselves, ideas cannot. Do not find common ground with these ideas, do not flinch when they are presented to you, and do not allow them to grow. You have the power to stop evil in your life. It is time to recognize the power we have and the true strength of our backbones.

Chapter 12

BECOMING A HERO IN A DANGEROUS WORLD

For believe me!—the secret for harvesting from
existence the greatest fruitfulness and the greatest
enjoyment is: to live dangerously! Build your cities
on the slopes of Vesuvius! Send your ships into
uncharted seas!...Soon the age will be past when you
could be content to live hidden in forests like shy deer!

—*Friedrich Nietzsche*

Why is it that when I talk to men in America and we discuss war or history, almost every single one of them says they dream of going back in time, fighting as a soldier in some great struggle? Some say they wish they could have fought in World War II against the Nazis, or they have fantasies about being a medieval knight, chivalrous and clad in armor on horseback. Some have visions of fantasy worlds where they are imbued with great powers and strength, ready to liberate some magical kingdom.

It is easy to write this off as just a boy's dreaming, but I believe there is something higher at work here. In every scenario that these men relay to me, it is almost always themselves presiding as the hero, where good triumphs over evil and the enemy is slain by the moral, the strong, and the brave. Dreams often reflect what we want in life, and the hero dream, as I call it, as a constant throughout human history shows exactly what our souls crave. We are designed to be heroes. It is in all of our hearts to take up our quest and govern our own existence. This doesn't mean violent action or setting out on your steed to faraway lands looking for a princess to save. It means building yourself as a hero, embracing danger, and setting your life story as an adventure.

The 1997 film *Princess Mononoke*, directed by Hayao Miyazaki, is one of my favorite movies of all time, right behind *The Lord of the Rings*. I have watched this film countless times, and am still enamored by its visuals, soundtrack, story, and characters. The movie tells the journey of a young man named Ashitaka, who after slaying a demon god of the forest who attacked his village is cursed by the beast and must depart west to find a cure for his ailment and see with eyes "unclouded by hate." During his quest, he comes in contact with two rival factions: the humans in Irontown, who create iron and guns using the resources of the forest, and the animal spirits and gods, who protect the forest. Both sides have needs and downfalls, and neither of the two is seen as inherently better or worse than the other. Lady Eboshi, the boss of Irontown, at first seems to be an arrogant, selfish capitalist with no regard for the spirits of the forest or the nature abounding around her. Yet when it is revealed that she buys brothel girls' contracts and takes in lepers to come to Irontown and escape their miserable lives, you see how she has given all of these "undesirables" safety, shelter, and privilege in her care.

The same is true for the animals, the spirit of the forest, and Princess Mononoke herself. It is easy to just think, "Nature good, people bad," like this was *Avatar* (a horrible film, by the way, totally overrated and nonsensical), but the animals and the princess are complete with their own faults, flaws, and misgivings. Many of them are solely full of hate, and act only in their own self-interest. This hatred leads to the death of the boar god and much of his clan, because he could not sensibly think of a better plan because his mind was so clouded by it.

Both sides in the war have moral failings, yet they also have admirable qualities. This sets them both into gray areas, where the movie doesn't pick sides between the two, it only chooses between bravery and cowardice, right and wrong, and good versus evil, and it does this through the eyes and heart of Ashitaka, the real hero of the film. Instead of joining the fray or instigating more division and pain between the two factions, Ashitaka serves on the side of both. He helps Lady Eboshi at the ironworks and helps defeat the Samurai attacking them, while also rescuing the princess and fighting alongside the wolf god to restore the spirit of the forest. He is a righteous hero at every stop along the way, and grows in his understanding of the world and right versus wrong throughout the film. He is humble, yet powerful and brave. He is helpful and masculine, and does many things seen as unpopular to both sides because he has no hatred. Both of the warring tribes despise Ashitaka for a time because they believe him to be on the other team, but their eyes clouded by hate can't reveal his true nature in his actions because they are consumed. It is not until the end of the film that the two sides see Ashitaka as the hero he is, and as he returns the head of the spirit of the forest to its body, potentially sacrificing himself in the process, his curse is lifted, and he is seen as a friend by both factions after the destructive war that has just taken place.

The moral conundrums that transpire between all parties in the film serve as a fable for the real world we live in. As you journey through life you will encounter lots of gray areas, and lots of tough choices and decisions to make. This experience can turn anyone cynical and make them think nothing is really good or bad and so it must all just be meaningless. But that is the coward's way of thinking, and the solution to cynicism and nihilism is adventure and heroism.

Ashitaka encapsulates everything it means to be a hero and

live dangerously. Other examples could be Sam from *The Lord of the Rings*, Don Quixote, Simba from *The Lion King*, Odysseus, and countless others. All heroes share similar characteristics and go through similar trials. There are also certain actions they must partake in to be considered heroes and not just someone who did one good or valiant thing.

Becoming a hero in the world today may seem like a daunting task from your air-conditioned bedroom. We have no great war, no dragons to slay, and the world has been almost wholly discovered and conquered. Our comfortable, easy lives make it seem like the hero's journey is a relic of the past, or only relegated to great people in movies and books. But that is a lie, twisted by the dark forces of this world to make you believe you are weak and not up to the task of being a hero. Molding your own life into a hero's journey and experiencing your days as if they are a quest is the path to fighting the nihilism and crisis of meaning that sweeps our nation and our souls. Until our people believe in the bravery inside them and that they are stronger, more creative, and more powerful than we have been led to think, we have no chance of saving our great country from the dragons that look to destroy us.

Your email marketing job does not make you a hero. The clothes you wear and how much you spent on them doesn't make you a hero. How much you drank last night or how many women you have been with does not make you a hero. How many followers you have on social media or how many likes your picture got does not make you a hero. This may all seem obvious, but many of our young people's insecurities and anxieties arise from a place of false heroism through vain and vapid means. They believe they are powerful because of fleeting bouts of pseudo-confident validation from others, but it is a ruse. It is a game devised by those at the top to give you a soft and false sense of self to keep you from becoming who you truly can be.

I myself know all about this type of lifestyle and arrogance. Seven years ago, as a twenty-year-old kid thrust into the spotlight with millions of video views, tons of followers, and money after being broke my whole life, I believed I was strong because of these things. For my first few years in politics I was vain and believed I had achieved much because of what our society deemed as status symbols of success. But I was no hero. I was merely a boy with pride who thought himself powerful by the standards of other people who were no heroes themselves. Once I looked to God and other people I thought were modern heroes as a source of leadership and conviction, I could untether myself from the hoax Will Witt I had constructed, and chart my new course. To start on your path to becoming a hero, you must abandon the false confidences you receive from solely pleasurable and meaningless artifices. Only then, when you release yourself from the hold of fake pride by entirely worldly confirmations of self, can you truly embark on your quest.

You must be ready to forsake your life as you know it to become a hero. Frodo could have stayed in the Shire and never taken the ring to Mordor. Simba could have stayed in the jungle with Timon and Pumba and never taken back his throne. At the beginning, it is quite easy to look at the daunting challenges ahead of you and refuse them out of fear and comfortableness. But risks are the only thing in life worth taking on. Do you survive, or do you live? Do you dream and act boldly, or do you blend in with the crowd? Do you ooze contempt and cynicism and watch your surroundings fall into despair, or do you make the world a better place and revive your soul? You must answer these questions honestly and believe in your answers before you set off to become a hero, or you will fail.

You may be reading this and have no idea where to even begin. To start your journey, you must answer your call. In the world today, there are plenty of admirable calls to venture into. It could be rescuing abused children around the world. It could be creating a wonderful family that you cultivate and lead. It could be becoming a warrior of God and preaching His message across the land. There are a myriad of callings all ready to be taken up, and you will know it is the hero's journey if it is a challenge. You cannot expect to achieve greatness for yourself, your family, or God if you do not do what is hard. You must be ready to face obstacle after obstacle and prepare yourself and your body and mind to overcome them, and you must be willing to incur much risk. The hero sets off on his quest with no guarantees he will return, and no certainty of success. It is called a risk for a reason. The hero makes no excuses for his failures, and he doesn't blame the world for the journey's outcome. You must be willing to face the dragon and slay it, or die trying. Most people would cower at the dragon, content with someone else going into the cave first to see what lies ahead. That cannot be you. You must be at the vanguard and accept that there are times in life where you will be separated from safety and pleasure, and that is a good thing.

Most people look at suffering and pain as a moral wrong.

That any time someone suffers or is hurt it must be a tragedy. This is how our schools raise children today. "Always be nice, look for peace, suffering is bad, risk is scary, hard work is unfair," they exclaim to the feeble youth. This could not be further from the truth. Instead of preparing children for a tough and dangerous world, we sugarcoat it and bubble-wrap them so that they are suffering-averse to the highest degree. A child should go through pain and difficulty to be aware of what lies ahead, but instead, we have neutered the youth of this country into soft weaklings who can't even take someone being mean to them on social media without breaking down into a full-scale panic attack. You cannot embark on the hero's journey if you are not ready for suffering. In fact, you should embrace suffering and welcome it into your life. Did you ever get out of a bad breakup and have someone tell you, "Well, at least you learned a lot from this relationship"? The words may not ring true in that moment in your hurt, but they are exactly what you should hear. You learn from the heartache, and strive for different priorities and outcomes next time with the newfound hardiness and knowledge you have obtained. Use the suffering and make it yours! Don't run away from it and don't suppress it.

Pain, toil, and hardship are the only way we grow and learn, and are the elixirs in a world dictated by the corrupt, selfish, and cunning. Instead of seeing the tyranny inflicted on us and hoping someone else saves us, why not have the courage to save ourselves and defeat them? As Nietzsche said, "What doesn't kill me makes me stronger." Use the diktats of the diabolical to make you into a hero, not into a slave. Take their wrath and use it as tinder for the fire you will use to defeat them. As the world closes in around you and the enemy tries to destroy you, take that pain and make it your shield, and rise above everything that falls. To make your life a heroic journey you must bring suffering into your life, and not shun it, but rejoice in it.

Suffering comes with sacrifice. The hero must be ready to sacrifice something to achieve his goals. If he is not willing to sacrifice anything, he cannot be a hero. One thing the hero must sacrifice is many of his relationships. I get asked all the time, "Will, I am a very strong Christian and want to stand up for my values, but I am afraid I may lose friends for what I believe. What should I do?" A lot of people I have heard, when asked this, try to give some politically correct answer, or tell them to put aside judgment and find common ground with one another as friends. I disagree completely. If living out your purpose in life, becoming a hero, and standing up for the kingdom of God makes you lose friends, then that is a good thing. It is an admirable thing. Separating yourself from those who are not looking for the hero's journey is how you grow stronger and more committed to goodness. You cannot expect people who have never challenged themselves for something greater than themselves in their lives to understand or congratulate you on your mission. Focus on your path, and the people who have the same passion and character will unveil themselves to you. As Galadriel says in *The Fellowship of the Ring*, "You are a ring-bearer, Frodo. To bear a ring of power is to be alone."

Heroes are many things, but above all else, they have integrity. They are ready to do the right thing even when no one else is watching. In your life, you will constantly be faced with choices in which you know the right answer, but the wrong answer is much easier, more convenient, or less painful. The secret to constructing a hero's quest as a life is to do your best to always act with integrity and be brave in the face of fear. Being afraid is normal. Second-guessing yourself is normal. Being dealt tough outcomes in life is normal. It is how you act in these situations and respond to them that sets you apart from the non-heroes and villains. No one will make the right choices all the time, and you, along with me and everyone else, will make mistakes and falter with your heroism and faith. But what you do after these setbacks is what defines the hero, and you can continue to strive for moral good even after you fail.

The last part of the hero's journey is their responsibility to others. You create your life as an adventure, you live dangerously, you are brave and chivalrous, and you are good, and now this new-found knowledge and power are to be used to help others and the world. Take what you learned and experienced and use it to send back into the universe all of what you know. You now have a calling to bring others on your journey and try and "disciple" them into heroes themselves. Being a hero and understanding more of the world and yourself should not make you arrogant, but instead a leader and a guide for others to follow. Build up others around you, and break free from envy and pride as the individual you have crafted yourself into.

A fictional work that perfectly exemplifies this concept is *The Lord of the Rings*, with its characters of Aragorn, Frodo, and Gandalf. All three of these men are idealized portrayals of masculinity and heroism, and each represents a different part of Jesus Christ.

Aragorn represents the king, Gandalf the powerful and the pilgrim, and Frodo the sacrifice. Aragorn, for example, as a male lead has uncommon attributes as a hero by today's standards. He is not a neutered man who is dominated by strong females, and he is not indecisive and weak. Yet he is also not an overtly tough and masculine character. He is not brutish or stubborn or some Andrew Tate–watching "Alpha Chad," unlike what we see so much of in today's media as the juxtaposition to the frail and feeble modern male archetype. Aragorn is chivalrous. He has developed skills and traits that he uses to defend the weak. He doesn't do this for himself, he does it because it is right. He treats every person with value, and his moral foundation does not push him to search for power over others, but instead power over himself and his own circumstances. He faces trial after trial, and although he is tested to his very limits he doesn't run away from his responsibilities. He instead seeks out evil and destroys it and is willing to sacrifice himself for the betterment of others.

Aragorn does not need to kowtow to others to be "likable" by today's standards, and he also doesn't have to be this toxic man we hear so much about. Aragorn is loved by the people of Middle Earth because *he* loves them. I find this to be such an important concept, and it is something to think about when you are watching the people who are presented as the "saviors" and heroes of our modern age. Is their mission to bring about change because they truly care and love the people they are trying to help, or is it born out of some insecurity within themselves or a desire to exert control over others? I am writing this before the results of his arrest and trial concerning allegations of rape and human trafficking, but someone like Andrew Tate and his opinions on manhood as a concept would appear outside looking in as a net positive for masculinity today. Yet I believe the only reason someone like Tate could receive so much popularity is that our world is so lacking in heroes and real masculinity.

Andrew Tate could step in and fill a need that was necessary, but the values he presents are not the values we really need. Andrew Tate does not love the world or the people he looks to change. Young men who have been shunned by their society and women look to someone like Tate as a leader and role model because they don't know any alternative. But there is a real alternative, and that alternative is chivalry, and it is becoming a hero. Chivalry is all of the ideals I have talked about in this chapter, and it is the antidote to the crisis of manhood we face. It is Aragorn risking his life to give Frodo the chance to destroy the one ring. It is Gandalf, a powerful spiritual being, being made approachable and helping the citizens of Middle Earth in their fight when he never was required to do so. It is Frodo bearing the paramount burden of humanity, making the ultimate sacrifice of his body and soul to destroy the ring for the rest of the world. That is what a hero is. It is not some boy who lets women walk all over him, who runs from danger and lives an easy life. It also is not some "man" who says "women ain't s——" and performs a life for their own vanity. It is someone who treats his position of power with reverence and responsibility, loves goodness and pursues it, and is willing to sacrifice everything of themselves for a higher truth.

Our world today sorely lacks heroes. It lacks role models for young people and mentors who want to teach. It lacks students who want to learn and people of great creativity. So many of the issues of today could be fixed by real leaders with godly goals and ambitions who educate and lead others to be leaders themselves. It is quite easy to look around and say, "Someone else can be that hero. I am just one person, so what can I really do?" The key here once again is that the hero doesn't know what the outcome of his journey will be. All he knows is what is right. And sure, you probably can't fix all the problems of the world and slay every dragon. But you can bring glory to God and yourself and give your life purpose. Our politicians aren't heroes, most wealthy CEOs aren't heroes, and the majority of people around us aren't heroes. Be the hero yourself that you would like to see everyone else be.

On the eve of battle in 1385, King John of Portugal spoke to his new knights: "Good my lords, this order of chivalry is so high and so noble, that he who is a knight should have no dealing with anything that is low, with vile things or with cowardice, but he should be as hardy and as proud as a lion in pursuit of his prey. And therefore it is my wish that this day you shall show such prowess as it befits you to show: that is why I have set you in the van of the battle. There so do that you may win honor; otherwise your spurs are not well set upon you." This is the bravery and honor we all should be striving for every day of our lives. Reject the mundane and easy, and embrace the hero inside you.

The world outside is perilous and full of monsters. Destructive politics, a selfish ruling class, false idols, nihilism, and hatred all aim to destroy the America we love. The country we grew up in is no longer here; will you be one of the heroes to help restore its former glory? Or will you stand idly by waiting for someone else to live out your quest? The choice is yours, but it starts with breaking away from the modern America and being brave in the face of all the danger Satan can muster to throw at you.

Chapter 13

THE MODERN AMERICA

It is difficult to write a paradiso when all the superficial indications are that you ought to write an apocalypse.

—*Ezra Pound*

I bet many critics reading this book may think what I have spoken about so far is egregious, or hyperbole, or simply lies. I have spent twelve chapters talking about the illnesses of the West and the perils it finds itself in, and many may be thinking, "Is it really all that bad?" or "Is he just trying to sell a fearmongering conservative book to get people riled up?" It is quite easy to look at America today and think the world is in pretty good shape. Medical innovation has saved millions of lives, and people rarely die from common diseases and ailments in this country anymore. The world is fed, and whatever information you would like to access at any time is constantly at your fingertips. You can communicate with anyone around the world at any moment, and the splendor around you is unparalleled. Everybody has exactly what they need, it would seem, so what is there to complain about? Well, a lot, actually, and the naïveté of thinking our world and psyches are safe is merely our modern and lazy pride speaking for us.

You may have technology at your fingertips. You may have food and pleasures aplenty. You may have a car, a house, and a job. But to the cultivated eye, our country is falling into decay, and these maladies are caused entirely by progress. Every time a man comes with a progressive new machine to institute into our society, it almost always regresses in unintended—or in the case of the world controllers, intended—ways. Our government has exploded in scope and bureaucracy, all in the name of progress.

Our churches have become relics of a religion and transformed into social clubs through progressive ideals. Our economy and markets have imploded on themselves in the name of creating something "better." Our universities and public schools have destroyed what it means to learn and have replaced it with obedience training and memorization serfdom, all in the name of creating a new and better education system. Progressivism is a locust that, once hatched out of its cocoon, cannot be sent back. It devours everything around it, pulverizing the landscape until nothing remains. Some may try and stop its invasion, but most just continue to let it be. Eventually all come to realize that a decimated crop is merely a symptom of the times, and think the solution to resowing the fields is unleashing more locusts, forgetting the cause of the famine in the first place. It is an endless cycle, and the locust feeds off the complacency and misgivings of the people, until one day the generations prior, who were the only ones to see the beauty of the land before the insect, have forgotten entirely how the world used to appear, and thus there is nothing to go back to, only forward, with more and more locusts spawned until the sky is blotted out with them, as the people herald them as a savior.

Progressivism destroys history. It destroys culture. It destroys human interaction. But most of all, it destroys hope and meaning in people. We are in a crisis of meaning in this country, where people are bred out of nihilism and subservient "civility" to a lazy and mediocre society. Let us take, for instance, how a modern Millennial is born, raised, and developed. First, they are coddled from the moment they are born. They are told the truth is subjective, and that even if they lose, they win; everyone gets a trophy just for taking part. They are told that equity and diversity trump all else, and that a meritocracy is unfair. In the case of young men, they are told that girlish behaviors are favorable, and are punished for acting like boys. They are sent to a school that teaches them nothing but how to recite facts, and then are plunged headfirst into a university that is nothing more than a daycare where they engage in every promiscuous vice imaginable, develop an addiction to alcohol and maybe drugs, and learn nothing of intrinsic value that will help them be courageous, critically thinking citizens. They move into the real world, working in some city, answering emails all day, working for some massive, soulless corporation, each monotonous task followed by another. They are tired and uninspired, so they drink and party with a bunch of people who feel just like them, never getting into serious relationships because social media has destroyed their concept of love and temptation. They watch mindless television and social media, content to pass the time, and have nothing in life they really strive for. They post on social media for some sort of affection and connection, but in the end it only fuels their insecurity. They can't afford a house because they are drowning in student loans and the government and corporations have destroyed the market to create a nation of renters. All in all, they feel hopeless. Everyone is the same, everyone belongs to everyone else, and everyone is manipulated by the world controllers.

Of course, not every young person's life is like this. But there is no denying that despite feeling like we have a plethora of choices in our society, we really only have two choices: find meaning, or live as a slave. Most choose the latter, because most don't even know they are a serf in the first place, mildly content with the small carving of existence they have. It is depressing indeed to hear this is the case, but we cannot fix the problem unless we first address it. Progress has done this to our young people, and in the striving to make things easier, more advanced, safer, and more decadent, we have erased a sense of purpose from millions of people, who now feel lost and distraught without a star in the sky to guide them.

In many respects, life goes on as it always has. You have railways and grocery stores, firefighters and ambulances. You can drive your car to work and read on your downtime. You can correspond with others and sit down with a glass of scotch and enjoy a piece of music. Yet despite the existence of these experiences, deep down you can feel it—there is a tremendous sickness in this country, isn't there?

With every passing day, the longing inside of all of us grows. Everywhere we go, the decay of the America we grew up in is apparent right in front of our eyes. Corruption and lawlessness. Conformity and mediocrity. Fear and weakness. Where once you had passion and bravery, you now have elites and bureaucrats dictating your compliance. Your elected officials have abandoned you, you are kept sick and dependent by pharmaceutical behemoths, and your speech is controlled by our new Big Tech overlords. In hopes of an escape we spend and spend on shiny new toys, and allocate our time to cheap dopamine hits through a screen. Our souls fester with the poison we consume, and we sleep away our dreams while we are still awake.

I know you can feel it. We all do. This is beyond our manufactured right versus left paradigm; it extends into our very humanity. The fires of creativity and wonder that burned in us as children are all but spent, and have extinguished themselves in the mundane and ordinary thrust upon us from every corner of our experience. Where once you had magnificent and revolutionary art, literature, and oration, you now have emails, tweets, and podcasts. The ideals and creations that at one time drove humanity forward have been all but forgotten, and have now been banished as relics and bygones. We have forgotten history, and thus we have forgotten beauty.

Beauty is a precarious thing, but it is achievable. For instance, what do you surround yourself with? It may sound like an obvious question; some of you may even be looking around your room right now thinking about possessions and objects you keep near you as your first answer. But what do you really surround yourself with? Do you surround yourself with staleness? Do you surround yourself with gray? Do you surround yourself with things that make you realize life is worth it? It can be difficult to know the answers to these questions, but one thing is for certain: The average Westerner's life is dominated by ugliness, vanity, numbness, and mediocrity.

Many things in this world have been ruined by modernity, but of course, many things have improved as well. Millions of people have been saved by medical advancements, the world has been fed, and the possibility of visiting distant planets is on the horizon. But what has happened to us humans in the process? As our modern world was born, the soul of man died and was left destitute, craving what it has longed for throughout the thousands of years of humanity.

Politics is ugly, social media is vain, and our world is held together by plywood and concrete. Everywhere you look is a reminder of the delusions of grandeur of our modern sympathies. Our music, movies, and art are at their best nothing more than cheap caricatures of the majesty of the past—and at their worst, a clear degradation of the world that built us. The buildings we call luxury are glass-and-steel monstrosities that jut viciously out of the earth, serving as a constant visage and emblem of our Tower of Babel arrogance. Our faces at night are emblazoned with the glow of ourselves as our screens bounce our fake personas back at us. The people elected and appointed to guide our world are nothing more than insecure goblins who feed off the pointlessness of the debate and who find their purpose through their own meretricious ambitions. Our cities and universities are steel boxes devoid of character with layouts akin to gaudy jail cells, where every vice can be satiated and mediocrity abounds. The forest is burned, and in its place comes a corporation's chasm of emptiness, familiarity, and blandness. Great thinking and writing and debate are replaced with the mundane and easy musings of lesser men. The outer world we experience ends up defining our lives and making us who we are, and for most of us, the experience is boring, ugly, and almost identical to everyone else's.

You have but one choice: Embrace beauty and search it out. There is much in life to be thankful for, yet many of us abandon the truly special events in our lives for ease and comfort. A beautifully handwritten letter, a majestic animal, a symphony of great caliber, the landscape of the country of your forefathers at sunset, a laugh from your child, a cathedral of splendor, an introspection about the world with the woman you cherish, the word of God: There is some beauty in this world, but it is up to you to find it. No one will give you the experiences your soul aches for, you must go and get them yourself. Abandon the comfortable similarities of others and revere your individuality. Find happiness where others are too lazy to look. Honor God and become a steward of the world around you. Love firm and true the ones who love you back. And give your heart to good things. Do not wade idly in the sea of this world, sweeping off to wherever the current takes you. Look around, breathe in its magnificence, and build your boat to voyage fiercely and bravely to the end of it all.

Beauty is one of three aspects needed to build a population of meaning. The three transcendentals, Beauty, Goodness, and Truth, are vital to a society with purpose. Goodness comes from more than just a battle with evil, as it is imperative to note that goodness is stronger than evil. Most people look at good versus evil as equals, but this is a fault. It can be easy to assume evil is as strong or stronger and more intoxicating even than the good, but this is due to the difficulty that comes with goodness. Goodness is hard, evil is easy. My former boss Dennis Prager always said that people are not born basically good. According to him, they are not created evil, just not good. Yet as I have thought more about this question I have come to the conclusion that it is less about being born with goodness or without than it is about being born with laziness. In almost every scenario, most people choose the path of least resistance, the wide road, if you will. They don't always intend to commit evil, or hurt others, or subject themselves to mediocrity, yet when the choice of hard good or easy evil is laid at their feet, they almost always choose the option that is most simple and frivolous. Choosing to consume your days with benign and menial tasks and activities is not evil, it is merely languorous and comfortable. Most of the time, people are not even concerned whether or not their decisions are for the betterment of the world or if they will hinder themselves or others, they simply act because it feels good, but doesn't necessarily do good. Hedonism, self-idolatry, and laziness can all be effortless. Goodness must be earned through diligence and perseverance. It is not something that is freely done, it must be achieved. That is why it can seem like the world around us is evil, when only small minorities of people make the hard decisions to guide themselves and society as a whole to the good. Without a population that understands difficult choices, that constantly selects ease and comfort, we cannot have a society of meaning. The world around us makes it very easy and safe to choose the evil option, but we must face all of our decisions head-on and choose righteousness and courage over mediocrity and sublime darkness.

We cannot have a society that functions without people actively looking for goodness, and the same is true for the truth. Just as evil is the easy option, so is a lie, and many times the two can be conflated. Today we live in a world consumed by lies. Thinking that a man can be born a woman is a lie, there is no way around it. It does not matter how you *feel*, or if you are an adult, or if you are dealing with some sort of trauma: In no circumstance is someone born the wrong gender; that is an unwavering fact. It is a lie that masks, social distancing, and lockdowns had a significant impact on preventing the spread of Covid, yet it is those lies that plunged the West into totalitarian, draconian chaos. It is a lie that all white people must be punished for the "sins" of their ancestors, and even more so that anyone's identity is predicated on their race, not on their actions. These are just three examples of such lies permeating our modern social lexicon, but how invasive they, and many more like them, have become in our society is unparalleled.

Let us look more in depth at the myth of people being born the "wrong gender." You can't go anywhere in America, visit any social media site, or even talk to anyone and not see or hear something about transgender people. It is absolutely everywhere, in every crevice of our society. Our society is now dominated by the transgender agenda, despite it affecting only a small portion of the population, and your views on it are now a litmus test to your being viewed as a noble or cruel person. Many people are swayed to speak the lies, even if they don't believe them, simply because they do not want to be ostracized for their viewpoints, and thus they commit themselves to lies for ease of group solidarity and a place of belonging free from ridicule. Yet when you sacrifice the truth here, you end up sacrificing a part of yourself. Every time you call a *he* a *she*, or use made-up pronouns, or submit to their agenda, you are becoming a liar. Sure, it would seem to be more compassionate in the moment to just go along with what people would like to be called, or to just accept what others tell you and stay quiet, but is it not actually *more* compassionate and helpful to say the hard truths? If someone is hurting themselves, do you enable them? Or do you tell them what they need to actually hear that no one else is brave enough to tell them? In that way, you are not made to lie, and that person can get the real assistance they need. If you don't tell the truth, then the lies will continue to get worse and worse. What started as a small group of adults who just wanted to say they are women despite being born men has now turned into the practice of removing the breasts of children in the name of "protecting" transgender kids. What a lie that is! When you give the liars an inch, they take a mile, and so those who preach the lies cannot be allowed to have their lies spread, infecting a population to the point where they no longer even know what the original truth was in the first place.

You can tell the truth with compassion. You can tell the truth with a good heart. You can tell the truth calmly. But if you are going to tell the truth, you must be bold, and you must harden and prepare your body and spirit for the consequences that come from the people who would see their or the world's lies preserved at all costs. To them, you are just a pawn to be captured on their road to dominion over your life and everyone's life around you.

This means, most importantly, telling the truth to yourself. I know this better than most, as I used to live a life dominated by lies. Throughout my freshman year of college, I was addicted to a lie. You see, during that time I was a shell of the man I am now. I drank all the time, I indulged in drugs and vices, I missed my classes out of sheer laziness, and I dishonored my family. I was depressed at the choices I was making, I didn't really have many great friends, I found confidence in the attention of the onlookers of my harrowing actions, and at times I wished I could just disappear, moving into a houseboat and fishing my days away alone. Yet despite my sadness, I continued down a path of misery and quick enjoyment and pleasures, and you know the worst part? I blamed everyone else for the ills of my world. I blamed my mom for not loving me enough and for being too hard on me. I blamed the people around me for being so sinful that they pushed me into my behavior. I blamed my grandparents for being too conservative and overbearing. I blamed my dad for getting sent to prison and leaving me with my mind full of trauma, causing me to act out. I lied to myself and everyone around me to compensate for the troubles and despair I got myself into.

It wasn't until I hit rock bottom that I realized I was lying. I flunked all my classes and basically lost a full year of college that I had to pay for with nothing to show for it but a bunch of guys who thought I was the coolest because I could shotgun a beer the fastest. For the next few years after that, I cleaned up my act. I still made a lot of mistakes, and still did a lot of stupid things, but I knew who was responsible for it when it happened now. I could not lie to the world and myself forever, and I had to make a change or suffer falling forever. It was only when I decided to live by truth and accept right and wrong that I could truly become someone who could aim for the other two pieces of the puzzle: goodness and beauty.

Truth is for yourself, yes, but it can be further cultivated through others and the sharing of the knowledge and honesty you have. The only way our country, our families, and our individual spirits survive is by always telling the truth, no matter what, and you cannot sacrifice it for anything or anyone. The greatest pursuit in our lives is the pursuit of truth, and through it, you can become a person you never dreamed you could be. I never believed I could be where I am now, or speak to thousands on grand stages, or write a national bestselling book, but I know the only way I was able to do it was through the truth, and even more importantly, the ultimate truth, God.

Our world is corrupted by ugliness, evil, and lies, yet when you peel back the layers corroding this world, you will see that these are more so complacency, comfort, and groupthink. The only way we fill the cup of meaning to the brim inside us is by finding Beauty, Goodness, and Truth again, and making the difficult choices to persevere despite the hardships we may face. What you will find in the end is that you are not defined or remembered by the easy decisions you make, but by the hard ones, and those, my friend, are the only ones worth making.

Chapter 14

GOD SAVE AMERICA

Men must be governed by God
or they will be ruled by tyrants.

—William Penn

G od is real, God is good, God is all-powerful, God is all-knowing, and God is the key to saving the West and ourselves. Everything I have discussed in this book so far has a practical solution, but they all fail without God. In a godless world, every matter solved is merely a door opened to another problem. Almost every issue we have as Americans derives from the lesser qualities of human nature, and no amount of think tank policy initiatives, campus speeches, influencer videos, or political theory discussions can save our souls. God is the only one with the power to do that, and thus He is the first and sole answer to the questions surrounding America's revival.

As many of you know, I used to be quite the atheist. I despised religion, and I loathed those who practiced it. It wasn't just a matter of not believing in God, it was almost a hatred of those who did. I saw happy little Christians believing in some fake otherworldly deity and scoffed at their naïveté. If someone told me they believed in God, I looked down on them. I thought of them as less intelligent, less cultivated, and less equipped to handle the hardship and evil of the world. How could someone who puts their faith in some false being made up by men thousands of years ago ever grapple with the reality of the plane of existence we live in and cope with the struggles of their lives?

I did not see God answering these people's prayers. The Christian cancer patients still died, the Jews still got in traffic accidents, and the Muslims still lost their children in childbirth. Where was God? Why wasn't He helping these people? If He was real, why would He let all of these horrific tragedies happen every day?

Why didn't God answer any of my prayers when I needed Him most?

I was born in 1996 in Denver, Colorado. Like most people, my earliest memories are made up mostly of bits and pieces of fragments of experiences. Yet there are some memories I remember incredibly vividly. In some cases, much too vividly.

At some point after I was born my mother and father got divorced, and so my sister and I split time between them. Sometimes I was with my mother, sometimes my dad, and sometimes my grandparents. We spent more time with my mother and grandparents, to be sure, but we also occasionally were sequestered to spend time with my father, who turned out to be a drunk and a drug addict. At the time I didn't know any of that, and I figured that he just had moments of exuberance that were more wild than other times. There were other people around in and out of the picture, some I knew briefly, others more at length. But it wasn't until about the age of thirteen when all my memories came back to me that I realized what those times really were.

In middle school I got in trouble for horseplay with one of my friends, and I ended up getting sent to the principal's office to receive my punishment. At first, sitting in that office chair alone, I was terrified of what was going to happen to me. Then I was worried about what my mom was going to think, and then, in what seemed like out of nowhere, I remembered being a child in bed.

After seven years, I suddenly remembered the sexual abuse I experienced at the hands of a man in my own family.

This person, in their own incoherence, abused me over and over again, and this flood of memories would change my life forever. At first as a thirteen-year-old nerdy kid with crooked glasses I experienced massive depression. I thought about killing myself all the time. I didn't sleep very well, a problem that still persists to this day. I would lie awake before bed thinking of the molestation, and then when I fell asleep my nights would be inundated with nightmares. I never told anyone any of this. My family knew about the abuse from the one time I mentioned it immediately after I first remembered, but it wasn't until 2022 that I ever talked to my mom about it again.

As I grew older, I coped with my abuse through vices and validation. Outwardly, I don't think anyone could see anything was awry inside my head, but I felt it all the time. I felt guilt and shame constantly, and to offset those feelings, I compensated by trying to make everyone around me like me, especially women. In my relationships with girls, I looked for validation of my self-worth above actual love, and couldn't ever really maintain a healthy connection with the other person. As soon as I received that validation from one woman who fell in love with me, it was on to the next. All of this is to say I haven't had a very steady life when it came to relationships, alcohol, or my own self-worth. I made a lot of stupid decisions, and none of what I was doing actually made me happy. Sure, I got bouts of confidence, but I felt empty as soon as the euphoric minute was over, and it was back to more of the same.

The reason I am telling this to you, the story I have never told in public before, is to show you why I was an atheist, and the truth of God. My abuse and my trauma *convinced* me not to believe in God. I wondered how God could have let this happen to me. How God could let me make such stupid choices. How unfair everything was in my life and how sad I could be. It is why I despised people who believed in God. How could *you* believe in God when this horrible thing happened to me?

Yet in the winter of 2021, after much self-reflection and faith, I got baptized in Hermosa Beach, California, in the cold ocean water. It was something I never thought I would do. In the midst of the Covid pandemic, being stuck at home, I decided to finally read the Bible and see what everyone was talking about. I ordered the text off Amazon, and when it was delivered, I read the four Gospels. What came next was a choice and a realization. I had now read the life of Jesus Christ and had the words of His sacrifice imprinted into my mind. At this point, as with any information presented to you, I had to make a decision. I could believe the text was full of lies, I could ignore it and disregard what I read, or I could believe it was true. But I was so moved by the words and the testimony within that there really was only one choice, and that was becoming a follower of Jesus Christ. If what is in those four Gospels is true, and Jesus Christ really was the son of God who died for my sins on the cross, then I had no other option but to give my life for Him. And so that is exactly what I did. It was the best decision I ever made.

If you would have told me in high school I would be a Christian/ conservative author and speaker, I would have punched you in the face. I was a proud atheist, Obama-loving, alcoholic teenager. No way could that ever be me! But in truth, God had bigger plans for me, and my baptism turned out to be the greatest day of my life.

But although I now was a Christian and had been baptized, I still struggled with my own issues and struggled with my faith. I had done therapy once or twice when I was younger, but I hated it, and I think I told my friends it was "for women." How's that for toxic masculinity? Granted, the field of psychology is full of pseudoscience, prescription drug addiction, and false prophets, but at the age of twenty-five I decided to try again, but this time with Christ at the center of my healing.

Anyone who has gone through intense trauma therapy will know just how straining it truly can be, and my therapy for my abuse was the hardest thing I have ever done. In many cases, the emotions and memories that came flooding back made me actually feel worse than ever before and tested me to my limit, reliving all the horror and abuse every day for months. I ended up getting diagnosed with PTSD from my trauma, and that almost destroyed me. But after long perseverance I ended up getting through the hardest part of my trauma work, and came out the other side with the sun still shining.

The key to my healing through these last few years has been Christ. The most important step and realization I came to with all this is understanding that you give yourself to Him, and instead of looking to yourself to solve all the problems of the world and your own soul, you just release it all to Him. Instead of making yourself your own savior, instead of carrying around shame and guilt from something that wasn't your fault, and instead of searching for worldly validation, you give it to Him. What is so ironic is that my original reason for being such a staunch atheist is now my biggest reason for believing in God. God gave me these challenges and struggles in my life to use me and make me the man I am. I look back on my hurt, my trauma, and my abuse now glad that it happened, and I wouldn't take what happened to me away for all the money in the world.

I can't say now that I am some perfectly healed man, free of sin and heartache, but I am trying my best every day. I know that God is with me even when I falter and that He will continue to heal me and guide me through everything I do, and that He will be and has been with me every step of the way no matter what.

God has the power to heal all things. God can heal America, and He can heal you. But it takes hard work for us to truly realize that and let Him in to do His work. What we face in America today is an unprecedented epidemic of weakness and godlessness. Sure, we have millions of people in America who go to church, who go through the motions of what a believer is supposed to be or who say they are a Christian, but what has faith in America turned into? Most churches are nothing more than social clubs, where you come in and get your free bagels, sing an *American Idol*–esque vocal performance with little substance or true conviction, and then get a tepid sermon from a pro-choice pastor who hung Black Lives Matter and Pride flags at his church. My pastor here in Tampa always says that if Jesus came back and set up a church next door to his, his church would still have more members because what we would ask of people is not what Jesus would ask

of them. Real faith and conviction is hard. The faith we have set-
tled with as Americans today is lazy and easy. What we are really
missing is the hard work and sacrifice it takes to be a believer.

Many people talk to me about their congregations and tell
me how they shouldn't have politics in their church, and that the
two should be separate. I disagree completely. For example, abortion is a political issue, but it is inherently a moral issue. It is the
murder of an innocent life, and thus it is a sin to commit abortion according to God. So abortion is evil and is the destruction
of human life, but because it is "political" your church shouldn't
talk about it? That doesn't make much sense to me. Or what about
the LGBTQ agenda sweeping the nation? God says marriage is
between a man and a woman, yet the issue has become entirely
political. Does this mean your church shouldn't talk about it? Or
should start doing gay weddings because it would be too "political" to not do them? Many churches across the country are far
more worried about saying the "wrong thing" by today's societal
standards than preaching the truth of the gospel. Once our pastors
start saying we can't be political, they are inherently sacrificing the
truth on biblical issues that have been politicized by man yet are
steadfast and unwavering truths in the eyes of God. Obviously not
every political issue is going to be directly congruent to biblical
teachings—you won't find tariffs and NATO in the Bible—but
many pastors would prefer to have a "big tent" congregation that
doesn't divide people or make them uncomfortable rather than a
church that actually teaches the word of God. This is a massive
fault. And what is worse is pastors using the words of the Bible
to push a message of absolving sinful behavior by misconstruing

biblical teachings for their own political gain. Yes, leftist pastor, Jesus Christ did love everyone, but He also called out evil and sin where He saw it, not just let it in and fester so people would think He was "with the times." "Jesus was a socialist" comes to mind as an example, or Christian churches in New York City hosting all-ages drag shows and justifying it by saying Jesus was "all about love." These are complete perversions of the teachings of the Bible and truly are the meaning behind taking the Lord's name in vain.

But what about separation of church and state? That must be what we strive for, right? Well, not exactly. Whenever someone says that phrase, I light up, because it means I get to ask them where in our founding documents the words "separation of church and state" are listed. Of course, most of them don't know, but in truth, it is a trick question. The phrase "separation of church and state" does not appear in our Constitution or Bill of Rights. Our First Amendment states, "Congress shall make no law respecting an establishment of religion, or prohibiting the free exercise thereof." That's it.

We have no state-organized religion here in America, and people can practice whatever religion they like, but what people get wrong about the founding fathers is that just because they wanted there to be religious freedom and no state church, that didn't mean they wanted an atheist people. John Adams said, "Our constitution was made only for a moral and religious people. It is wholly inadequate to the government of any other." Benjamin Rush, a signer of the Declaration of Independence, said, "The only foundation for a useful education in a republic is to be laid in religion. Without this there can be no virtue, and without virtue there can be no liberty, and liberty is the object and life of all republican governments. Without religion, I believe that learning does real mischief to the morals and principles of mankind." George Washington said, "Religion and morality are the essential pillars of civil society." Sure, Thomas Paine wasn't much of a religious guy, but for the secularists to come out in droves claiming there was no religious framework behind the U.S. Constitution and republic is a farce.

The founding fathers of America were brilliant men. What the Enlightenment brought with its values of liberty, justice, freedom, and truth, many atheists took as a win for godless societies. Although the Enlightenment did change people's perceptions of religion as a whole and brought with it many consequences that would define our modern world, the founding fathers used Enlightenment beliefs in conjunction with biblical truths to create America. America was not just some idyllic, Enlightenment paradise that put knowledge, equality, and liberty above all else. It was an experiment of those values that the founding fathers knew could only be possible with God's will and a population of people that had faith in God. This is why the American Revolution worked, and why many of the constitutions of the French Revolution failed. The French tried to destroy the church, whereas the American founding tried to elevate it.

We have been led to believe in our prevailing atheist culture that the separation of church and state is morally superior. It is now almost an automatic cancellation online and an extremist view to even utter the thought that maybe separation of church and state isn't such a great thing, despite this being the case for hundreds of years in Europe during many of the decades that defined what the West really is. I am not here arguing for a state church joined with the American government, but I find it ridiculous how stigmatized even thinking about it is. I can already see the atheist reviewers reading this book and tweeting, "Will Witt wants to start a Christian theocracy in America where gays are flayed in the streets." All for the simple reason that I asked a question about it. The fact that you can't talk about it in today's day and age should tell you everything you need to know.

If you go around the world and see the struggles Christians deal with on a daily basis, it would make any American Christian feel guilty for their lapse of faith and work. In some parts of China, people are not allowed to celebrate Christmas, one of the most important Christian holidays. Along with Uyghur Muslims, some Christians in China are taken to what can only be described as concentration camps, where they are tortured for their belief in Jesus Christ. Those who refuse to denounce their faith are treated terribly, and are oftentimes killed for their faith. Yet despite death and punishment, many of them still refuse to denounce their beliefs. In Indonesia, pastors' heads are cut off and placed on spikes outside their churches to intimidate believers. In the Middle East, Christian women have acid thrown on them for their beliefs and Christian businesses are burned down solely for the fact they are owned by Christians.

I met a refugee pastor from the Middle East (I cannot say his name, where I met him, or the country he was from due to concerns over his safety), who had made it to America after spending ten years in one of the harshest and most hellish prisons in the world, where he was tortured on a daily basis for his preaching and work as a pastor. He escaped to America, and he told me his story while sitting down for breakfast. Once he had finished telling me all the horrors he had been through, I asked him what his plan was next. Would he preach in America? Would he lobby Congress for help in his country? Would he lay low and remain hidden after what they had done to him?

No, it was none of the above. In fact, he told me he was going back to the country where he was imprisoned, to continue to spread the word of Jesus Christ despite the likely probability he would be tortured again or, worse, killed. This man's story inspired me incredibly. This was someone who was not afraid of other people, with such a strong conviction to go and put himself in horrible danger to evangelize and preach. This man was my hero because he feared God far more than he feared the wrath of other people.

Contrast this with America, where I talk to Christians in the states who say, "Yeah, I guess I'm a believer," or "I don't talk about my faith," or "I'm embarrassed of what people will think if I tell them I'm a Christian." I find it almost laughable when I hear these responses, especially the last one, which after talking to hundreds of people across the country I hear much more than you would expect. Romans 6:23 says, "For the wages of sin is death, but the free gift of God is eternal life in Christ Jesus our Lord." So what these people are telling me is that although the greatest gift in the world that could be bestowed upon them has been given to them for free, they are afraid to tell people about it because they are *embarrassed*? Give me a break. People around the world are dying every day for their faith, yet you are too embarrassed of what some blue-haired girl in your sociology class is going to think of you for professing your love of God? No one is saying you need to be visiting the most dangerous places in the world and preaching to the masses, but if you are too scared to even say you are a Christian living in a country where your freedom of speech is protected by law, you need to take a look in the mirror and reevaluate your beliefs and priorities. Embarrassment because of what others believe about your faith comes not from God, but from a lapse in your own convictions about your faith.

Now, I get why people would feel ashamed. We live in a post-Christian society in the West in many respects, and "science and technology" have been presented as the antidotes to a "brainwashed, religious world." There is much shame and shunning from atheists who look to put believers down for the sole reason that they are believers (remember, I was one of these people), but your faith must be more steadfast and hardier than the insults others throw at you. It cannot be merely a branch on your tree that can easily be cut down and discarded. Your faith must be your roots and your foundation. Jesus told us all that we would be persecuted for our faith, and if you are not ready for that, or believe it is "unfair" that people don't like you for your strong convictions, then once again, it is time to reevaluate your beliefs and think about why you are a Christian. Are you a Christian to feel like you are a part of a group or to bring you happiness in *this* material life? Or are you a Christian because you know God is real and Jesus suffered and died for *your* sins on the cross? There is a massive difference there, and it is up to us to think of that for ourselves. Imagine if we had a spiritual army of millions of that second group of people, what we could accomplish in this country. Well, that is my aim and what I would one day love to do, and it is far more important than every political debate we could ever have.

It is easy to think we no longer need God, and that religion is a relic of the past. Western medicine has saved countless lives, modern agriculture has massively helped curb world hunger, and other technologies have altered the human experience forever in ways that seem to turn us into our own type of gods, but the issue is thinking that God and these technologies and innovations are unrelated. This is all according to God's plan, and all happens for a reason, according to Him.

Many people will say we don't need God due to the fact that we are already morally *good*. The commandment "do not murder" is redundant to many because according to them we are already bound instinctively to shun murder and believe it is wrong without God or the Bible. Most of these people have never read history. Just take a look at the ancient Aztecs, who sacrificed children and cut their hearts out of their still-living bodies. They saw this as a moral good, and necessary to appease their gods. But this is evil. If you believe that evil is subjective and up to each person's interpretation, then what the Aztecs did could be considered great. What Hitler, or Stalin, or Mao did could be considered beautiful or heroic to some. But that is not the reality of the world, and we know indubitably that these acts and events are objectively evil only because of God and biblical truth. Without Him, all actions are morally gray and subjective, and up to any person's own opinion on whether they are right or wrong. People need God's word to know the truth about what actions and ways are right and wrong, otherwise we devolve into acts of brutality and evil.

This is the crux of all of this. It is the crux of this whole book, all politics, all discussions you could ever have, and every decision in the world. The fact of the matter is that the number one goal of the elite ruling class in this country is to destroy God and the Bible, make it irrelevant, and convince people it is a sin in this brave new world to be a believer in Christ. If the elites destroy God, then they destroy truth, which means objective truth is abandoned entirely, which means they get to be the new gods of the land and justify any action as *moral* in their eyes, because who else dictates morality but them? This is how our leaders get away with such evil, such greed, and such selfishness: because they convince the people that *their* truth is the only way forward, without a second thought to what God might think about it. And then a weakened and neutered Christian population, along with an atheistic skeptic culture, goes along with whatever the oligarchy professes because it is easy, everyone else around them believes it, and they don't know enough about the real truth to think critically on what they have been presented with. There is a reason Karl Marx despised God and why Soviet Russia outlawed religion: because when people really knew God's truth, they could no longer be convinced of the ruler's lies.

The information, facts, arguments, and lessons in this book all amount to this. Every chapter discusses an issue in our society or in our culture or human nature, and every issue is subverted on its head by the rulers of this country to make you believe all truths are subjective, and that someone like me calling the elites evil is merely a matter of opinion. Sushi tasting disgusting is a matter of opinion. Red as your favorite color over green is a matter of opinion. But a selfish dictatorship in disguise subduing your capacity to think clearly, turning you into a serf, stripping you of your inalienable rights, and attempting to destroy God and truth in our world *is* evil, there is no doubt about that.

I know not everyone reading this will be a Christian, or may have never even thought about God past going to church on Sunday every so often. But this is the true nature of the world and ourselves that we cannot deny any longer, unless we would like a world bereft of anything that could be seen as objective. You will be hard-pressed to find even atheists who disagree with the fact that if everyone followed the Ten Commandments, the world would be a better place. We must be evangelical with our beliefs and be good stewards of the truth to advance these values, and that comes with responsibility and sacrifice.

I hear people always asking, "When will the world change?" "When will our politics change?" "When will America change?" But I never hear people asking, "When will *I* change?" We are constantly expecting things to get better in our world, or to become "fair" or honest, but that is not the world we reside in. It is not the world any human being has ever resided in. We live, as did our ancestors, in a world of constant sin, manipulation, terror, and loss. If we solved every issue today, the world would become cursed again tomorrow. It is human nature. We are constantly looking for the world to fix itself without first trying to fix ourselves. We blame the world for every malady when we ourselves are not living to the best of our ability. For me, with all my trauma, insecurities, mistakes, and problems, I had to look deeply at myself and put healing and changing as a priority in my life. I could have blamed my circumstances or the world or other people, and even though the world and others weren't blameless in my life, it was still up to me to overcome the challenges I faced and be a better person than what the world served to me, and I could only do this through Christ. The key to our existence on this earth is to overcome the foul aspects of our nature and live as most akin to Christ as possible.

You will not be able to change the world in its entirety and create a utopia. Communism and Nazism were attempts to create utopia on earth, and they utterly failed and destroyed the lives of millions of people. But what you can do is honor God and improve yourself, striving for truth, goodness, and beauty with all that you achieve. You can become a hero and influence the lives of others in a positive way. You can appreciate fantastic art and tradition and create majesty around you. You can remove yourself from toxic modern standards of living. You can change your media and tech habits and pursue what is real and honest. You can improve your diet and your health and build your body and spirit together firmly. You can become a true free thinker and disregard the musings of those who try to shun you for the way you choose to live and what you know to be right. You can stop trying to placate the masses of evil and instead unwaveringly stand up for morality, hope, and virtue. You can become self-sufficient and stop predicating your identity on whatever political topic is popular that day. You can cover yourself in the armor of God and fight for Him, becoming the embodiment of a warrior of truth. And you can become an individual again, and find that not complying means more than mandates or leftist talking points. It means not complying with what the elites want you to feel. Nihilism, poor health, immorality, victimhood, godlessness, vanity, distractions, ugliness, hatred, cowardice, and groupthink are all a manner of complying. Do not comply with any of them.

The man of today has become the antithesis of humanity. His future is being hijacked and his past is being distorted by elites who understand through all modes and any means necessary how to make us their slaves. They have contorted us into puppets, holding the strings as they dance us around. Is that the existence you choose to live? Blind and obedient to another's power games of control? Will you be the slave? Or will you be the master of your own life and fight for truth while doing it? To retake our souls, our humanity, and our faith we have but one choice, as difficult and tumultuous as it may seem: Do not comply. The greatest views are only able to be seen once you scale the mountaintop, and I pray that we are all never content again with the visions below, but only rest once we have reached the apex.

Chapter 15

COURAGE IS FOUND IN UNLIKELY PLACES

"Go back?" he thought. "No good at all! Go sideways?
Impossible! Go forward? Only thing to do! On we go!"
So up he got, and trotted along with his little sword
held in front of him and one hand feeling the wall,
and his heart all of a patter and a pitter.

—*J. R. R. Tolkien, The Hobbit*

Courage! Is there anything more noble than courage? Courage is the antidote to fear, as you can only be courageous when you are afraid.

Humans make up to thirty-five thousand decisions every day.[1] Every choice you make in life presents you with the potential for bravery, no matter how innocuous you may think it is. The evanescent nature of our options at any moment makes most things we do seem trivial, yet when we look back, we can clearly see how every choice we have made has led us to where we are now. You have all the power in the world now to combat the daily fears you face and make decisions that will bring you to the pinnacle of your potential. You must be conscious, you must be hardy, and you must put first the good values you know to be true.

I did not want to write this book as just another "Republican" book. I wanted to write something that could be accessible to anyone, and would help people break free from the groupthink and nihilism we have trapped ourselves in. We are more than what we have become. I am not talking here about the drama between conservative media companies, or the Twitter clips of Republicans in office that only serve themselves. These things are merely diversions to keep you inundated with cheap content and mindless distractions from what our focus should really be set on. If our lives were a movie, the elites, politicians, and influencers would be the stars playing their roles, and we would be listed as mere extras in the credits. Are you content with just being the extra? Or do you leave the theater and direct your own film? Do you let these elites keep you blind and dumb as a mindless consumer? Or do you stand against the tyranny and idolatry of our age and seek out what others won't?

I wrote this book because I am fearful of what our world is transforming into, and what we are losing. People often ask me if I am hopeful for America and the West, and with a straight face, I usually tell them no. I hate to say it, but I see our country sequestered by lunacy, degeneracy, corruption, and laziness. But because of this state that our world is in, I am more hopeful than ever for the future, because only in such dire circumstances as these can great men rise to meet the occasion and be truly heroic, spectacular people. I am assured now more than ever that a small group of people will uphold the tenets of goodness and truth and become more than what little achievement the masses are content with having. There is great ambition and courage within all of us, and that flicker of a flame of a future we envision is kindling inside you. You just have to tend it and keep it burning without letting the winds of the outside world put it out.

They say that if you lose something, the best thing to do to find it again is to stop searching. We are constantly looking for answers for how we can fix this country, but we are searching in all of the wrong places. We must stop expecting power structures, or human nature, or leftism, or technology, or elites to change. We must change, we must fight, we must pursue truth, and we must be courageous. What you will find is that when you are brave, and when you change with the power of God, the unlikely place you were looking for answers might just have the remedy to finding what you have lost. The solution to the American crisis is not external, it is within, and the answer lives inside all of us.

Believe me when I say that I lose faith in the world, but I do not lose faith in *you*. You have more power than you know, and you are stronger than you realize. Never stop learning, never stop teaching, never stop pursuing curiosity, and never stop your courage. The world is filled with evil, your life is filled with sin, and everyone is flooded with doubt. Do you let this stop you? Or do you not comply in the face of all fear and madness and climb out of the fiery chasm of our potential future? The choice is yours, my friend.

Every day is a test, but every day is a blessing. The next day may be harder than the last, but the only days worth having are the ones with great struggle and triumph. It might seem hopeless at times, but I promise: Within the darkness, there is light. There is some good in this world, my friend, and it is worth fighting for.

ACKNOWLEDGMENTS

A plethora of people helped me create this book, and I am incredibly grateful for all of them. I couldn't have done this without all of their help and wisdom.

First, I would like to thank Dennis Prager for writing the foreword of this book and for everything he has taught me. Many of the values and ideas I discuss in this book would never have appeared on these pages without Dennis, and his wisdom and knowledge have been some of the greatest inspirations in my journey from boy to man. Dennis was always there to help me no matter what, no matter how busy he was, and no matter the Jewish holiday, and I am honored to call him a great friend and mentor.

I also would like to thank all of the people at Hachette/Center Street who made this book possible. Alex, Katie, and Daisy have all been incredibly helpful every step of the way in this book's creation and distribution, and I couldn't have had a better team in making it.

Esther, Danielle, and everyone else at the Fedd Agency were also incredibly helpful in bringing the idea of this book to life, and when the world around me kept saying NO, Esther continually said YES and made everything I've done possible.

The biggest thank-you this time around I must give is to my grandfather Chocolate, who I dedicated my last book to. He passed away in the spring of 2022, and with his passing I lost my best friend in the whole world. Chocolate was everything a man should be, and loved like every grandfather should love. He was wise, blunt, kind, funny, hardworking, and reverent, and above everything, he believed in me like no one else. I am indebted to him for the rest of my life, and without him I probably never would have made it.

Thank you to my mom for always telling me that even if she didn't agree with my politics, she at least liked my outfits in my videos. I love you, Mom, and am so appreciative for all the support you have given me and how you are always there for me. Thank you for everything.

Thank you to my stepdad, Bob, for always driving me forward and believing in everything I was doing. Thank you to my grandmother Cookie, who I would always have long political discussions with and hammer down all my ideas. She pushed me to make my arguments and presentations the best they possibly could be and never let me get away with mediocrity.

Thank you to my sister, Maddy, for being my best friend and rock, especially these last few years as I've gone through these trials and hardships. She is always there for me and challenges me when I need it, and although she always loses to me in Ping-Pong, she always gets back up to play again and is stronger than anyone I know. Thank you to my brother, Zach, as well, who was my best friend growing up and taught me to question everything.

I also would like to thank Dr. Jeff Barke for helping me create chapter 3 on Big Pharma. His writing and research are what made that chapter possible, and he is truly an amazing friend and mentor. Dr. Jeffrey Barke is a board-certified primary care physician in private practice for over twenty-five years. He completed his medical school and family practice residency at the University of California, Irvine. He has served as an associate clinical professor at UC Irvine and a board member of the Orange County Medical Association. Dr. Barke is the author of *COVID-19: A Physician's Take on the Exaggerated Fear of the Coronavirus*. Dr. Barke is a proud founding member of America's Frontline Doctors. He is also the cohost of the podcast *Livin the Good Life*. His website is www.RxForLiberty.com.

Thank you to my friend Jake Buol, who helped me research this book, and is one of the most trustworthy and genuine guys I know. Thank you to Alex Guerra, who moved out to Florida with me and helped me start *The Florida Standard*, for always dealing with all my stubbornness and antics and for being the guy I know I can always turn to. I also have to thank Jacob Hansen, who has been my friend for the last twelve years and is the most dependable person I've ever met. All of my friends have been my rocks while I was writing this book, and were there to challenge, push, and help me through this, and everything else.

Thank you to everyone at PragerU, especially Craig and Marissa. They are the ones who took the chance on me all those years ago and made me what I am today, and although I don't work for PragerU anymore, I still love them all and appreciate more than anything what they did for me, even if Craig is a little too feminine of a boss.

Acknowledgments

Thank you to my therapist, who I won't name here, but who has become one of my closest friends and confidants, and who taught me that real healing comes from Christ, not any worldly means. Without you, there is no way I ever would have realized where I was, or where I needed to go. I love you, thank you.

My final thanks is for Jake English, who I dedicated this book to. A man who has no ulterior motive to help me other than the fact that he cares about me and believes in me like no one else. Jake, you have been my greatest friend and helper these last few years and I don't deserve how great you are to me. From the bottom of my heart I hope you know how thankful I am for you, and how much you mean to me. In many ways, you are the father I never had, and I love you for everything. Thank you for always being there for me when it seemed like no one else was, and I promise I won't forget any of it. Let's celebrate this book with a cigar and a whiskey at your place. I'll even bring the Indian food this time.

NOTES

INTRODUCTION
AMERICAN REALITY

1. "Social Changes," Encyclopædia Britannica, www.britannica.com/place /ancient-Rome/Social-changes.
2. Garrett M. Petersen, "Rome's Economic Suicide with Lawrence Reed and Marc Hyden," The Economics Detective, February 15, 2016, https:// economicsdetective.com/2016/02/romes-economic-suicide-lawrence -reed-marc-hyden/.
3. "Panem and circenses," Wonders of the World, www.wonders-of-the-world .net/Colosseum/Panem-et-circenses.php.
4. N. S. Gill, "Economic Reasons for the Fall of Rome," ThoughtCo., July 1, 2019, www.thoughtco.com/economic-reasons-for-fall-of-rome-118357.
5. Annalisa Merelli, "1,700 Years Ago, the Mismanagement of a Migrant Crisis Cost Rome Its Empire," Quartz, May 7, 2016 https://qz.com /677380/1700-years-ago-the-mismanagement-of-a-migrant-crisis-cost -rome-its-empire.
6. "The US States Spending the Most on Welfare," Commodity.com via *Roanoke Times*, September 22, 2021, https://roanoke.com/lifestyles /the-us-states-spending-the-most-on-welfare/collection_32a3bdb8-67bc -5b4a-ab63-36c146adaed3.html#1.
7. Christopher Chantrill, "US Welfare Spending for 2023—Charts," USGovernmentSpending.com, December 6, 2020, www .usgovernmentspending.com/us_welfare_spending_40.html.
8. "Department of Defense Spending Profile," USAspending.gov, November 29, 2022, www.usaspending.gov/agency/department-of-defense?fy=2023.
9. Emily Cochrane, "The Senate Passes a Spending Bill That Includes Nearly $50 Billion in Aid for Ukraine," *New York Times*, December 23, 2022, www.nytimes.com/2022/12/23/world/europe/the-senate-passes-a -spending-bill-that-includes-nearly-50-billion-in-aid-for-ukraine.html.

10. "The Impact of Illegal Immigration on the Wages and Employment Opportunities of Black Workers," April 4, 2008, www.usccr.gov/files /pubs/docs/IllegImmig_10-14-10_430pm.pdf; Bill Melugin and Adam Shaw, "Fox News Footage Shows Mass Release of Single Adult Migrants into US," Fox News, January 27, 2022, www.foxnews.com/politics /texas-footage-single-adult-migrants-released-us.

11. Hans von Spakovsky, "Federal Report Shows Open Borders Bring Increased Crimes and Costs for Taxpayers," Heritage Foundation, December 12, 2021, www.heritage.org/immigration/commentary /federal-report-shows-open-borders-bring-increased-crimes-and-costs -taxpayers.

12. William La Jeunesse, "Most Illegal Immigrants in US Receive Government Benefits, Costing Taxpayers Billions: Experts," Fox News, April 22, 2019, www.foxnews.com/us/the-cost-of-illegal-immigration -migrants-cost-us-taxpayers-billions-a-year.

13. Jenna Ross, "Pedophilia in Ancient Greece and Rome," The Collector, May 24, 2020, www.thecollector.com/pedophilia-ancient-greece-rome/.

14. Brian Flood, "Washington Post Slammed for 'Normalizing,' 'Minimizing' Pedophilia: 'Part of the Depravity,'" Fox News, January 9, 2023, www .foxnews.com/media/washington-post-slammed-normalizing -minimizing-pedophilia-they-have-become-part-the-depravity.

15. Victor Davis Hanson, *Dying Citizen: How Progressive Elites, Tribalism, and Globalization Are Destroying the Idea of America* (New York: Basic Books, 2022).

16. Irina Ivanova, "Millennials Are the Biggest—but Poorest—Generation," CBS News, November 26, 2019, www.cbsnews.com/news/millennials -have-just-3-of-us-wealth-boomers-at-their-age-had-21/.

17. Alyssa Schukar, "'Playing Catch-up in the Game of Life.' Millennials Approach Middle Age in Crisis," *Wall Street Journal*, May 20, 2019, www .wsj.com/articles/playing-catch-up-in-the-game-of-life-millennials -approach-middle-age-in-crisis-11558290908?mod=article_inline.

18. Chris Nichols, "Fact-Check: Have One-Third of US Small Businesses Closed During Pandemic?," *Austin American-Statesman*, June 8, 2021, www.statesman.com/story/news/politics/politifact/2021/06/08/kamala -harris-small-business-closures-covid-fact-check/7602531002/.

CHAPTER 1
A BRAVE NEW WORLD

1. Nathan Yerby, "Addiction Statistics," Addiction Center, September 22, 2022, www.addictioncenter.com/addiction/addiction-statistics/.

2. Ron Manderscheid and Paul Samuels, "1 In 3 Americans Is Affected by Addiction or Mental Illness: We Need a Plan to Protect Their Care," *The*

Hill, March 10, 2017, https://thehill.com/blogs/congress-blog/healthcare
/323334-1-in-3-americans-is-affected-by-addiction-or-mental-illness-we/.

3. Lydia Saad, "What Percentage of Americans Drink Alcohol?," Gallup,
December 28, 2022, https://news.gallup.com/poll/467507/percentage
-americans-drink-alcohol.aspx.

4. Werner Geyser, "The Real Social Media Addiction Stats for
2022," Influencer Marketing Hub, August 3, 2022, https://
influencermarketinghub.com/social-media-addiction-stats/#toc-19; Maya
Kosoff, "Study: 420 Million People Around the World Are Addicted to the
Internet," Business Insider, December 20, 2014, www.businessinsider
.com/420-million-people-are-addicted-to-the-internet-study-2014-12.

5. Lance DeHaven-Smith, *Conspiracy Theory in America* (Austin: University
of Texas Press, 2016).

CHAPTER 2
AMERICA'S POLITICAL SYSTEM

1. Barbara Wolff, "Was Declaration of Independence Inspired by Dutch?,"
University of Wisconsin–Madison, June 29, 1998, https://news.wisc.edu
/was-declaration-of-independence-inspired-by-dutch/.

2. Robert Higgs, *Crisis and Leviathan: Critical Episodes in the Growth of
American Government* (New York: Oxford University Press, 1987).

3. "Top Recipients of Contributions from Lobbyists, 2022 Cycle,"
OpenSecrets, accessed November 8, 2022, www.opensecrets.org/federal
-lobbying/top-recipients.

4. "Lobbying—the Good, the Bad and the Ugly," Open Source
Investigations, September 17, 2020, www.opensourceinvestigations.com
/democracy/lobbying-the-good-the-bad-and-the-ugly/.

5. Peter Eavis, "How FedEx Cut Its Tax Bill to $0," *New York Times*,
November 19, 2019, www.nytimes.com/2019/11/17/business/how-fedex
-cut-its-tax-bill-to-0.html.

6. Joel Friedman, "The Decline of Corporate Income Tax Revenues," Center
on Budget and Policy Priorities, October 24, 2003, www.cbpp.org
/research/the-decline-of-corporate-income-tax-revenues.

7. "Policy Basics: Federal Payroll Taxes," Center on Budget and Policy
Priorities, October 25, 2022, www.cbpp.org/research/federal-tax/federal
-payroll-taxes.

8. Auberon Herbert, *The Right and Wrong of Compulsion by the State, and
Other Essays*, ed. Eric Mack (Indianapolis: Liberty Fund, 1978).

9. Ella Nilsen, "Capitol Hill's Revolving Door, in One Chart," *Vox*, June 19,
2019, www.vox.com/2019/6/19/18683550/capitol-hill-revolving-door
-in-one-chart.

10. "Man Who Killed Republican Teenager over 'Political Argument' Is Free on Bail," *Washington Free Beacon*, September 22, 2022, https://freebeacon .com/latest-news/man-who-killed-republican-teenager-over-political -argument-is-free-on-bail/.

CHAPTER 3
BIG PHARMA

1. Spencer Lindquist, "Pharma Co. Creates Feminizing Drugs, Sponsors Pro-Trans Film for Children," Breitbart, November 11, 2022, www .breitbart.com/social-justice/2022/11/12/pro-transgender-propaganda -film-for-children-sponsored-by-pharmaceutical-company-that-creates -feminizing-drug/; "Mama Has a Mustache Documentary," Mama Has a Mustache, accessed February 5, 2023, www.mamahasamustache.com/.
2. Zachary Rogers, "'Mama Has a Mustache': Pharma Giant Partners with Gender Discussion Film for Children," The National Desk, November 15, 2022, https://thenationaldesk.com/news/americas-news-now/pharma -giant-bayer-sponsors-gender-discussion-film-for-children-mama-has -a-mustache-diane-rubin.
3. "Dosage Form and Strength: Cyproterone Acetate 2,0 Mg plus Ethinylestradiol 0,035 Mg per Tablet," Bayer, July 21, 2022.
4. Spencer Lindquist, "Company That Produces Puberty Blockers Backs Pro-Trans Children Group," Breitbart, July 18, 2022, www.breitbart .com/health/2022/07/18/company-under-investigation-puberty-blockers -sponsors-pro-trans-children-organization/.
5. Lisa Raffensperger, "Drug Used to Halt Puberty in Children May Cause Lasting Health Problems," STAT, February 2, 2017, www.statnews .com/2017/02/02/lupron-puberty-children-health-problems/.
6. Spencer Lindquist, "Puberty Blocker Company Paid Co-Director of Children's Gender Clinic," Breitbart, July 26, 2022, www.breitbart .com/health/2022/07/26/puberty-blocker-company-paid-co-director -childrens-transgender-clinic/.
7. "Leading Lobbying Industries U.S. 2021," Statista, accessed December 7, 2022, www.statista.com/statistics/257364/top-lobbying-industries-in -the-us/.
8. Aimee Picchi, "Drug Ads: $5.2 Billion Annually—and Rising," CBS News, March 11, 2016, www.cbsnews.com/news/drug-ads-5-2-billion -annually-and-rising/.
9. Brooklin Nash, "Pharma Is Growing Its Digital Ad Spend. But by How Much?," Media Radar, March 10, 2021, https://mediaradar.com/blog /pharma-digital-ad-spend-growing/.
10. Zachary Brennan, "Do Biopharma Companies Really Spend More on Marketing Than R&D?," Regulatory Affairs Professionals Society (RAPS),

July 24, 2019, www.raps.org/news-and-articles/news-articles/2019/7/do
-biopharma-companies-really-spend-more-on-market.

11. Anthony Farris, "Pfizer Apparently Sponsors Everything on Mainstream
Media," OutKick, October 21, 2021, www.outkick.com/pfizer-apparently
-now-sponsors-everything-on-mainstream-media/.

12. "Biden Administration Paid Hundreds of Media Outlets with Taxpayer
Money to Spread Covid Vaccine Propaganda," *Rio Times*, March 10, 2022,
www.riotimesonline.com/brazil-news/modern-day-censorship/biden
-administration-paid-hundreds-of-media-outlets-with-taxpayer-money
-to-spread-covid-vaccines-propaganda/.

13. Tom Breen, "Why Is the FDA Funded in Part by the Companies It
Regulates?," UCONN Today, May 21, 2021, https://today.uconn.edu
/2021/05/why-is-the-fda-funded-in-part-by-the-companies-it
-regulates-2/.

14. Erin Banco, "How Bill Gates and Partners Used Their Clout to Control
the Global Covid Response—with Little Oversight," *Politico*, September
14, 2022, www.politico.com/news/2022/09/14/global-covid-pandemic
-response-bill-gates-partners-00053969.

15. Janice Hopkins Tanne, "Royalty Payments to Staff Researchers Cause
New NIH Troubles," PubMed Central (PMC), January 22, 2005,
www.ncbi.nlm.nih.gov/pmc/articles/PMC545012/.

16. George Fareed, "Covid-19 Mass Casualties Due to Suppression of Early
Treatment by Dr. George Fareed," *Desert Review*, April 8, 2022. www
.thedesertreview.com/multimedia/covid-19-mass-casualties-due-to
-suppression-of-early-treatment-by-dr-george-fareed/html_e2cb919a-b775
-11ec-8c60-8fb6373a5fa9.html.

17. Fabien Deruelle, "The Pharmaceutical Industry Is Dangerous to Health.
Further Proof with COVID-19," PubMed Central (PMC), October 21,
2022, www.ncbi.nlm.nih.gov/pmc/articles/PMC9610448/.

18. Alex Ledsom, "France Bans Hydroxychloroquine to Treat COVID-19,"
Forbes, May 27, 2020, www.forbes.com/sites/alexledsom/2020/05/27
/france-bans-hydroxychloroquine-to-treat-covid-19/?sh=231a893821ab.

19. Association of American Physicians and Surgeons (AAPS), "Researchers
Overdosing COVID-19 Patients on Hydroxychloroquine, States
Association of American Physicians & Surgeons (AAPS)," June 17, 2020,
www.prnewswire.com/news-releases/researchers-overdosing-covid-19
-patients-on-hydroxychloroquine-states-association-of-american
-physicians--surgeons-aaps-301078986.html.

20. Jacob Puliyel, "Dose Related Toxicity of Hydroxychloroquine," *BMJ*,
February 9, 2023, www.bmj.com/content/370/bmj.m2670/rr-1.

21. Yanis Roussel and Didier Raoult, "Influence of Conflicts of Interest on
Public Positions in the COVID-19 Era, the Case of Gilead Sciences," *New*

Microbes and New Infections 38 (November 2020), www.sciencedirect.com /science/article/pii/S2052297520300627.

22. Ibid.

23. Jon Cohen, "The 'Very, Very Bad Look' of Remdesivir, the First FDA-Approved COVID-19 Drug," *Science*, October 28, 2020, www .science.org/content/article/very-very-bad-look-remdesivir-first-fda -approved-covid-19-drug.

24. J. V. Chamary, "The Strange Story of Remdesivir, a Covid Drug That Doesn't Work," *Forbes*, November 9, 2022, www.forbes.com/sites /jvchamary/2021/01/31/remdesivir-covid-coronavirus/?sh=37bd788066c2.

25. Francesco Guarascio, "EU Makes 1 Billion-Euro Bet on Gilead's Covid Drug Before Trial Results," Reuters, October 13, 2020, www.reuters.com /article/us-health-coronavirus-eu-remdesivir/eu-makes-1-billion-euro -bet-on-gileads-covid-drug-before-trial-results-idUSKBN26Y25K.

26. "Widows Suing Inland Empire Hospitals for COVID-19 Treatments Involving Remdesivir," CBS Los Angeles, October 25, 2022, www .cbsnews.com/losangeles/news/widows-suing-inland-empire-hospitals -for-covid-19-treatments-involving-remdesivir/.

27. Spencer Kimball, "What's Next for Pfizer, Moderna Beyond Their Projected $51 Billion in Combined Covid Vaccine Sales This Year," CNBC, March 3, 2022, www.cnbc.com/2022/03/03/covid-pfizer -moderna-project-51-billion-in-combined-vaccine-sales-this-year.html.

28. "Similac Sensitive Infant Formula Ready-to-Feed, 1Qt Bottle, Case of 6," Similac, accessed December 7, 2022, www.similac.com/products /baby-formula/sensitive-ready-to-feed/1qt-bottle-6pack.html.

29. Kris Gunnars, "Are Vegetable and Seed Oils Bad for Your Health?," Healthline, December 12, 2019, www.healthline.com/nutrition/are -vegetable-and-seed-oils-bad.

30. Alan Sherzagier, "Drug Companies Forge Partnerships with Top Schools," MPR News, January 13, 2013, www.mprnews.org/story/2013/01/13 /drug-companies-forge-partnerships-with-top-schools.

31. Laura Hensley, "Big Pharma Pours Millions into Medical Schools—Here's How It Can Impact Education," Global News, August 12, 2019, https:// globalnews.ca/news/5738386/canadian-medical-school-funding/.

32. Art Van Zee, "The Promotion and Marketing of Oxycontin: Commercial Triumph, Public Health Tragedy," *American Journal of Public Health* 99, no. 2 (February 2009): 221–27, www.ncbi.nlm.nih.gov/pmc/articles /PMC2622774/.

33. Jan Hoffman, "Purdue Pharma Is Dissolved and Sacklers Pay $4.5 Billion to Settle Opioid Claims," *New York Times*, September 1, 2021, www .nytimes.com/2021/09/01/health/purdue-sacklers-opioids-settlement.html.

34. Fabien Deruelle, "The Pharmaceutical Industry Is Dangerous to Health. Further Proof with COVID-19," PubMed Central (PMC), October 21, 2022, www.ncbi.nlm.nih.gov/pmc/articles/PMC9610448/.

35. Richard Smith, "Medical Journals Are an Extension of the Marketing Arm of Pharmaceutical Companies," PubMed Central (PMC), May 17, 2005, www.ncbi.nlm.nih.gov/pmc/articles/PMC1140949/.

36. Ibid.

37. "Big Pharma Is Buying Your Favorite Supplement Brands: Here's What You Need to Know," Next Health, July 11, 2022, www.next-health.com /blogs/news/big-pharma-is-buying-your-favorite-supplement-brands -here-s-what-you-need-to-know.

38. Joseph Marcela, "Big Pharma Wants to Put an End to Vitamins and Supplements," *Epoch Times*, July 19, 2022, www.theepochtimes.com /health/big-pharma-wants-to-put-an-end-to-vitamins-and-supplements _4606826.html.

39. Shane Starling, "Food Supplements Are Safest Foodstuffs: Report," Nutraingredients.com, July 10, 2012, www.nutraingredients.com /Article/2012/07/11/Food-supplements-are-safest-foodstuffs-Report.

40. Suneil Agrawal and Babak Khazaeni, "Acetaminophen Toxicity," NCBI Bookshelf, August 1, 2022, www.ncbi.nlm.nih.gov/books/NBK441917 /#:~:text=It%20is%20responsible%20for%2056%2C000,is%20contained %20in%20combined%20products.

41. Jacqueline Howard, "What Is Rainbow Fentanyl? Colorful Pills Drive New Warnings About Deadliest Drug in the US," KCRA, September 25, 2022, www.kcra.com/article/what-is-rainbow-fentanyl/41375131#:~:text =The%20CDC's%20latest%20provisional%20data,the%20year %20ending%20March%202022.

42. Justin McCarthy, "Big Pharma Sinks to the Bottom of U.S. Industry Rankings," Gallup, November 20, 2021, https://news.gallup.com /poll/266060/big-pharma-sinks-bottom-industry-rankings.aspx.

43. Arielle Bosworth, "Price Increases for Prescription Drugs, 2016–2022," Assistant Secretary for Planning and Evaluation, Office of Health Policy, September 30, 2022, https://aspe.hhs.gov/sites/default/files/documents /d850985c20de42de984942c2d8e24341/price-tracking-brief.pdf.

44. Mike Leonard, "Mylan $264 Million EpiPen Price-Gouge Deal Gets First Court Nod," Bloomberg Law, March 14, 2022, https://news .bloomberglaw.com/antitrust/mylan-264-million-epipen-price -gouge-deal-gets-first-court-nod.

45. Rina Torchinsky, "'Pharma Bro' Martin Shkreli Has Been Released from Prison," NPR, May 19, 2022, www.npr.org/2022/05/19/1100019063 /pharma-bro-martin-shkreli-been-released-from-prison.

46. Christopher Gerry, "Why Americans Hate Big Pharma More Than Ever," American Council on Science and Health, September 9, 2019, www.acsh .org/news/2019/09/09/why-americans-hate-big-pharma-more-ever-14275.

47. Susannah Luthi, "AbbVie Sued over Humira 'Patent Thicket,'" Modern Healthcare, March 19, 2019, www.modernhealthcare.com/politics-policy /abbvie-sued-over-humira-patents-blocking-competition.

48. Eric Sagonowsky, "Allergan Was Blasted for Its Unusual Mohawk Patent License, and Now It's a Total Flop," Fierce Pharma, February 26, 2018, www.fiercepharma.com/legal/allergan-s-controversial-tribal-licensing-pact -falls-short-ptab-scrutiny.

49. Sharon Yadin, "Shaming Big Pharma," *Yale Journal on Regulation*, November 9, 2019, www.yalejreg.com/bulletin/shaming-big-pharma/.

CHAPTER 4
BIG TECH

1. Joseph Mercola, Ronnie Cummins, and Robert Francis Kennedy, *The Truth About Covid-19: Exposing the Great Reset, Lockdowns, Vaccine Passports, and the New Normal* (White River Junction, VT: Chelsea Green Publishing, 2021).

2. Matt Taibbi, "1. THREAD: The Twitter Files THE REMOVAL OF DONALD TRUMP Part One: October 2020-January 6th," Twitter, December 9, 2022 https://twitter.com/mtaibbi/status /1601352083617505281.

3. Ibid.

4. Bari Weiss, "THREAD: The Twitter Files Part Two. Twitter's Secret Blacklists," Twitter, December 9, 2022, https://twitter.com/bariweiss /status/1601007575633305600?lang=en.

5. Matt Taibbi, "1. Thread: The Twitter Files, Part Six TWITTER, the FBI Subsidiary," Twitter, December 16, 2022, https://twitter.com/mtaibbi /status/1603857534737072128.

6. Michael Shellenberger, "1. Twitter Files: Part 7 The FBI & the Hunter Biden Laptop How the FBI & intelligence community discredited factual information about Hunter Biden's foreign business dealings both after and *before* The New York Post revealed the contents of his laptop on October 14, 2020," Twitter, December 19, 2022, https://twitter.com /shellenbergermd/status/1604871630613753856.

7. David Zweig, "1. Thread: the Twitter Files: How Twitter Rigged the Covid Debate—By censoring info that was true but inconvenient to U.S. govt. policy—By discrediting doctors and other experts who disagreed—By suppressing ordinary users, including some sharing the CDC's *own data*," Twitter, December 26, 2022, https://twitter.com/davidzweig /status/1607378386338340867.

8. Alex Horton, "Channeling 'The Social Network,' Lawmaker Grills Zuckerberg on His Notorious Beginnings," *Washington Post*, December 5, 2021, www.washingtonpost.com/news/the-switch/wp/2018/04/11 /channeling-the-social-network-lawmaker-grills-zuckerberg-on-his -notorious-beginnings/.

9. Will Duffield, "Repealing Section 230 Would Limit Americans' Speech," February 6, 2021, Cato Institute, www.cato.org/commentary/repealing -section-230-would-limit-americans-speech.

CHAPTER 5
BIG MEDIA

1. Kyle Spencer, "Inside the Far-Right's Fight for College Campuses," *Rolling Stone*, November 28, 2022, www.rollingstone.com/politics/politics -features/raising-them-right-far-right-fight-college-campus-1234636392/.

2. "Time Magazine's Most Surprising People of the Year," Sky HISTORY, accessed December 23, 2022, www.history.co.uk/articles/time-magazine -s-most-surprising-people-of-the-year.

3. Charlotte Hsu, "How Media 'Fluff' Helped Hitler Rise to Power," University at Buffalo, August 28, 2015, www.buffalo.edu/news/releases /2015/08/034.html.

4. David Folkenflik, "'The New York Times' Can't Shake the Cloud over a 90-Year-Old Pulitzer Prize," NPR, May 8, 2022, www.npr. org/2022/05/08/1097097620/new-york-times-pulitzer-ukraine -walter-duranty.

5. Ashley Lutz, "These 6 Corporations Control 90% of the Media in America," Business Insider, June 14, 2012, www.businessinsider.com /these-6-corporations-control-90-of-the-media-in-america-2012-6?op=1.

6. Dan Froomkin, "*The Washington Post* Has a Bezos Problem," *Columbia Journalism Review*, September 27, 2022, www.cjr.org/special_report /washington-post-jeff-bezos.php.

7. Jerusalem Demsas, "Wall Street Isn't to Blame for the Chaotic Housing Market," *Vox*, June 11, 2021, www.vox.com/22524829/wall-street-housing -market-blackrock-bubble.

8. Adam Johnson, "Comcast-Owned Vox Explains the Great Deal You're Getting from Comcast," FAIR, April 12, 2017, https://fair.org/home /comcast-owned-vox-explains-the-great-deal-youre-getting-from-comcast/.

9. "Board of Directors," BlackRock, accessed January 27, 2023, https:// ir.blackrock.com/governance/board-of-directors/default.aspx.

10. Howard Kurtz, "When Fake News Goes Viral: Lessons of a Lie About Ivermectin," Fox News, September 9, 2021, www.foxnews.com/media /fake-news-viral-lessons-lie-ivermectin.

CHAPTER 6
AMERICA'S FINANCIAL INSTITUTIONS

1. G. Edward Griffin, *The Creature from Jekyll Island: A Second Look at the Federal Reserve* (Thousand Oaks, CA: American Media, 1994).
2. Seymour Morris Jr., *Fit for the Presidency? Winners, Losers, What-Ifs, and Also-Rans* (Lincoln, NE: Potomac Books, 2017).
3. Lyn A. Schwartzer, "Money-Printing: 2020 vs. 2008," SeekingAlpha, November 4, 2020, https://seekingalpha.com/article/4384862-money -printing-2020-vs-2008.
4. Alex Hudson, Rakim Brooks, and Mark Davis, "The World Is $277 Trillion in Debt So Why Aren't Economists More Worried?," *Newsweek*, November 24, 2020, www.newsweek.com/world-277-trillion-debt-so -why-arent-economists-more-worried-1549818.
5. Pedro Nicolaci da Costa, "A Glaring New Conflict of Interest Undermines Public Trust in Federal Reserve," *Forbes*, May 7, 2020, www.forbes.com /sites/pedrodacosta/2020/04/20/a-glaring-new-conflict-of-interest -undermines-public-trust-in-federal-reserve/?sh=31f52f43135d.
6. Jon Fleetwood, "Company That Owns All Mainstream Media, Covid VAX Manufacturers Approaches $10 Trillion in Assets," American Faith, November 24, 2021, https://americanfaith.com/company-who-owns -all-mainstream-media-covid-vax-manufacturers-approaches-10-trillion -in-assets/.
7. Charlie Gasparino, "BlackRock's Larry Fink Rattles Employees amid Political Posturing," Fox Business, January 25, 2019, www.foxbusiness .com/business-leaders/blackrocks-larry-fink-rattles-employees-amid -political-posturing.
8. Jeannette Cooperman, "How a Company Called BlackRock Shapes Your News, Your Life, Our Future," Common Reader, September 14, 2021, https://commonreader.wustl.edu/how-a-company-called-blackrock-shapes -your-news-your-life-our-future/.
9. David Dayen, "Another BlackRock Veteran Will Join the Biden Administration," *American Prospect*, January 6, 2021, https://prospect.org /cabinet-watch/another-blackrock-veteran-will-join-biden-administration -michael-pyle/.
10. Cezary Podkul, "Fed Hires Blackrock to Help Calm Markets. Its ETF Business Wins Big," *Wall Street Journal*, September 18, 2020, www.wsj .com/articles/fed-hires-blackrock-to-help-calm-markets-its-etf-business -wins-big-11600450267.
11. "Our Mission," World Economic Forum, accessed January 27, 2023, www.weforum.org/about/world-economic-forum.

12. Jill Krasny, "Every Parent Should Know the Scandalous History of Infant Formula," Business Insider, June 25, 2012, www.businessinsider.com /nestles-infant-formula-scandal-2012-6.
13. "Leadership and Governance," World Economic Forum, accessed January 14, 2023, www.weforum.org/about/leadership-and-governance.
14. "List of Public Figures (R129)—World Economic Forum," accessed January 14, 2023, www3.weforum.org/docs/WEF_AM22_List_of _confirmed_PFs.pdf.
15. Klaus Schwab, "Now Is the Time for a 'Great Reset,'" World Economic Forum, June 3, 2020, www.weforum.org/agenda/2020/06/now-is-the -time-for-a-great-reset/.

CHAPTER 7
TRANSHUMANISM AND THE FUTURIST MOVEMENT

1. Natalie Winters, "EXC: Apple, Amazon, Microsoft Attended Chinese Communist Party's AI Conference Alongside Chinese Military Proxies," The National Pulse, July 30, 2020, https://thenationalpulse.com/2020 /07/29/apple-amazon-microsoft-ccp-ai-conference/.
2. "Elon Musk's Neuralink Brain Implant Could Begin Human Trials in 2023," Forbes, December 7, 2022, www.forbes.com/sites/qai/2022/12 /07/elon-musks-neuralink-brain-implant-could-begin-human-trials-in -2023/?sh=59f9f0dd147c.
3. Gareth Tyson, "A First Look at User Activity on Tinder," Queen Mary University of London, July 7, 2016, www.eecs.qmul.ac.uk/~tysong/file /Tinder.pdf.

CHAPTER 8
THE DESTRUCTION OF ART

1. Julia Marsh, "Thomas Jefferson Statue Removed from City Hall After 187 Years," New York Post, November 23, 2021, https://nypost.com/2021/11 /22/thomas-jefferson-statue-leaves-city-hall-after-187-years/.
2. "Statue of Abraham Lincoln with Kneeling Slave Removed in Boston," Associated Press via Fox News, December 29, 2020, www.foxnews.com /us/statue-of-abraham-lincoln-with-slave-kneeling-removed-in-boston.

CHAPTER 9
THE INDIVIDUAL VERSUS THE COLLECTIVE

1. Christopher R. Browning, Ordinary Men: Reserve Police Battalion 101 and the Final Solution in Poland (New York: Harper Perennial, 1992).

CHAPTER 10
THE BEAUTY OF UNPOPULAR OPINIONS

1. Timothy Ballard, *The Lincoln Hypothesis: A Modern-Day Abolitionist Investigates the Possible Connection Between Joseph Smith, the Book of Mormon, and Abraham Lincoln* (Salt Lake City: Deseret Book, 2016).
2. Erika Holst, "'One of the Best Women I Ever Knew': Abraham Lincoln and Rebecca Pomeroy," *Journal of the Abraham Lincoln Association* 31, issue 2 (Summer 2010): 12–20, https://quod.lib.umich.edu/j/jala/2629860.0031 .204/--one-of-the-best-women-i-ever-knew-abraham-lincoln?rgn =main%3Bview.
3. "The Civil War and Emancipation," PBS, accessed January 27, 2023, www.pbs.org/wgbh/aia/part4/4p2967.html.
4. Rachel Goldstein, "Three Things You Didn't Know About the American Revolution," University of Rochester, News Center, April 20, 2021, www.rochester.edu/newscenter/three-things-you-didnt-know-about -the-american-revolution/.
5. Joshua Young, "Trans Activist Gets Woman Fired from Video Game Company for Crime of Following Ian Miles Cheong, Libs of TikTok on Twitter," *Post Millennial*, January 8, 2023, https://thepostmillennial .com/trans-activist-gets-woman-fired-from-video-game-company-for -crime-of-following-ian-miles-cheong-libs-of-tiktok-on-twitter.
6. Sophia Narwitz, "Oh wow, the cancel crusading brony thinks young teens can consent to sex with an adult. It's almost as if this is a repetitious theme among those who cling to the cancel culture bandwagon the hardest," Twitter, January 8, 2023, https://twitter.com/SophiaNarwitz/status /1612166778620186626?ref_src=twsrc%5Etfw%7Ctwcamp %5Etweetembed%7Ctwterm%5E1612166778620186626%7Ctwgr %5E2265857b5d2cc545219e6b6147b52a54e7df6720%7Ctwcon %5Es1_&ref_url=https%3A%2F%2Fthepostmillennial.com %2Ftrans-activist-gets-woman-fired-from-video-game-company -for-crime-of-following-ian-miles-cheong-libs-of-tiktok-on-twitter.
7. Douglas Blair, "12 People Canceled by the Left After Expressing Conservative Views," Heritage Foundation, September 20, 2021, www .heritage.org/progressivism/commentary/12-people-canceled-the-left -after-expressing-conservative-views.

CHAPTER 11
NO COMMON GROUND WITH PEOPLE WHO HATE US

1. David Satter, "100 Years of Communism—and 100 Million Dead," *Wall Street Journal*, November 6, 2017, www.wsj.com/articles/100-years-of -communismand-100-million-dead-1510011810.

CHAPTER 15
COURAGE IS FOUND IN UNLIKELY PLACES

1. Frank Graff, "How Many Decisions Do We Make in One Day?," PBS North Carolina, August 10, 2022, www.pbsnc.org/blogs/science /how-many-decisions-do-we-make-in-one-day/.

ABOUT THE AUTHOR

Will Witt is a media personality, international speaker, short film and documentary director, and cultural commentator. He is the author of the national bestselling book *How to Win Friends and Influence Enemies*. He lives in Tampa where he's the editor in chief of *The Florida Standard*.